A B C
OF
AIRPORTS
AND
AIRLINERS

By
O. G. Thetford

LONDON

Ian Allan Ltd

1948

Left: American Overseas Airlines Lockheed Constellation NC 90925 *Flagship America.*
A.O.A. operates seven Constellations on the New York-London services.

Centre Upper: American Overseas Airlines Skymaster *Flagship Shannon* NC 90910 arriving from New York.

Centre Lower: A Douglas Dakota of Aer Lingus at Northolt.
Below: Douglas Dakota F-BAXA, one of thirty-six Dakotas operated by Air France on European routes.

(Photos: A. S. C. Lumsden

2

INTRODUCTION.

SINCE the Ministry of Civil Aviation first made available the Public Enclosures at Britain's major airports the attendance figures have been increasing by leaps and bounds and it is now sufficiently clear that not only the young aircraft enthusiasts but many members of the wider public are finding interest and relaxation in this form of pastime. Indeed, there can be few people of any age who fail to be fascinated sooner or later by the spectacle of airliners of all nationalities arriving and departing with clockwork regularity. It is not so very long ago since the crossing of the Atlantic by air or a flight from England to Australia earned front-page headlines in every newspaper. Nowadays, within the space of an hour at London Airport, the spectator can see Constellations from India, Australia, South America and New York, Canadairs from Montreal, Skymasters from South Africa and Yorks from the Gold Coast. Likewise at Northolt, clustered on the arrival apron at any time of the day there are airliners from Sweden, Switzerland, Italy, Holland, Greece, Eire and Czechoslovakia.

No spectator however can have his entire interest aroused unless he has some understanding and knowledge of the events he is witnessing and the supply of such needful information is a facility lacking at most airports. The present handbook it is hoped will satisfy this requirement. In preparing it, the author's intention has been twofold, inasmuch as it aims at equal interest for the knowledgeable professional spotter and the average uninformed member of the public.

The enthusiast will find that it lists for the first time the registration letters and individual aircraft names of the fleets of every airline company operating into the British airports, and includes photographs of all current types of airliners in the livery of every company. In obtaining the photographs I have had the co-operation of Mr. Alec S. C. Lumsden of the British Air Line Pilots' Association, to whom I wish to take this opportunity of expressing my thanks. Mr. Lumsden's enthusiasm in the task has been unbounded and his keen appreciation of the collector's requirements is, I think, adequately reflected in the rarity-value of many of the pictures.

In addition to the foreign airliners, the entire fleets of the three British airline corporations are, of course, listed, and there is also

3

a check list of British charter companies operating multi-engined aircraft with details of the fleets. Charter aircraft fall generally into the airliner class and as in the course of their multifarious duties they are likely to be seen at any airport at any time, it has been thought advisable to include them.

The reader approaching the book innocent, in the main, of things aeronautical, will find that there is included an "A to Z" list of the registration letters of every scheduled airliner liable to be seen at any airport in the British Isles, which identifies at a glance the type and nationality of the aircraft and the company to which it belongs. To promote further a knowledge of the different types of aircraft there is a set of outline recognition drawings, accompanied by notes of general interest and what the Americans usually describe as " pertinent data " relating to every airliner type currently operating on scheduled air routes.

Of direct utility to both categories of reader is the section devoted to the various airports, arranged alphabetically from Aberdeen (Dyce) to Southampton (Eastleigh). This section contains tables listing times of arrival and departure of the various companies' services and also stating the point of departure or alternatively the destination of the aircraft. The times quoted are those of the official summer schedules issued by the airline companies concerned and the frequencies are in most instances liable to reduction after October, though the routes operated remain unchanged. The map provided for most of the airports shows clearly the layout of the administrative buildings and the direction and length of the runways.

In conclusion, I wish to offer my thanks to Mr. Charles W. Cain who, in his capacity as Editor of "The Aeroplane Spotter", granted his permission for the publication in this book of the various silhouettes appearing in the section devoted to the description of the current types of airliners in service.

O. G. T.

July, 1948.

AIRLINES OPERATING SERVICES TO AND FROM THE BRITISH ISLES

Company Name	Nationality	Year Founded	Airports Used in U.K.
A.B. Aerotransport ..	Swedish	1919	Northolt Prestwick
Aer Lingus	Irish	1936	Northolt Manchester Liverpool Renfrew Dublin Shannon
Air France	French	1933	London Manchester Prestwick Shannon
Air India International ..	Indian	1948	London
Alitalia	Italian	1947	Northolt
American Overseas Airlines	American	1942	London Prestwick Shannon
British European Airways Corporation	British	1946	Northolt Aberdeen Belfast Blackpool Edinburgh Liverpool Manchester Renfrew Ronaldsway
British Overseas Airways Corporation	British	1940	London Prestwick Shannon Southampton
British South American Airways Corporation ..	British	1946	London
Central African Airways	Rhodesian	1946	London
Ceskoslovenske Aerolinie (C.S.A.)	Czech	1946	London Northolt
Cie Air Transport ..	French	1946	Croydon Gatwick
Cobeta	Belgian	1947	Manchester Prestwick

5

Company Name	Nationality	Year Founded	Airports Used in U.K.
Det Danske Luftfartselskab (D.D.L.)	Danish	1918	Northolt Prestwick
Det Norske Luftfartselskab (D.N.L.)	Norwegian	1919	Northolt Prestwick
Flota Aerea Mercante Argentina (F.A.M.A.) ..	Argentine	1946	London
Hellenic Airlines ..	Greek	1947	Northolt Prestwick
Iberia	Spanish	1930	London
Icelandic Airways ..	Icelandic	1944	Prestwick
Iraqi Airways	Iraqi	1945	London
Koninklijke Luchtvaart Maatschappij (K.L.M.)	Dutch	1919	London Manchester Prestwick Dublin
Luxembourg Airlines ..	Luxembourg	1947	Northolt
Pan American World Airways	American	1927	London Prestwick Shannon
Panair do Brasil	Brazilian	1930	London
Qantas Empire Airways ..	Australian	1934	London
South African Airways ..	South African	1931	London
Sabena	Belgian	1923	London Dublin Shannon
Scandinavian Airlines System	Merger of D.D.L., D.N.L. and A.B.A.	1946	Northolt Prestwick
Swissair	Swiss	1922	London Northolt Shannon
Trans-Canada Airlines ..	Canadian	1937	London Prestwick Shannon
Trans - World Airlines (Registered as Transcontinental and Western Air Inc.)	American	1930	Shannon

A.B. AEROTRANSPORT FLEET.

(Component of Scandinavian Airways System).

DOUGLAS DC-6 CLOUDMASTERS.

SE-BDA	Agnar Viking		SE-BDF	Alvar Viking
SE-BDB	Agne Viking		SE-BDL	Ambjörn Viking
SE-BDC	Alf Viking		SE-BDM	Anund Viking
SE-BDD	Algaut Viking		SE-BDO	Arngrim Viking
SE-BDE	Alrek Viking			

DOUGLAS DC-4 SKYMASTERS.

SE-BBA	Sigtrygg Viking		SE-BBE	Svavar Viking
SE-BBC	Sigvard Viking		SE-BBF	Sverker Viking
SE-BBD	Styrbjorn Viking		SE-BBG	Not yet named

DOUGLAS DC-3 DAKOTAS.

SE-BAA	Arne Viking		SE-BBH	Helge Viking
SE-BAB	Bele Viking		SE-BBI	Ivar Viking
SE-BAC	Folke Viking		SE-BBK	Kare Viking
SE-BAL	Lage Viking		SE-BBL	Loke Viking
SE-BAS	Sture Viking		SE-BBM	Magne Viking
SE-BAT	Torbjörn Viking		SE-BBN	Nore Viking
SE-BAU	Ubbe Viking		SE-BBO	Orvar Viking
SE-BAW	Vidar Viking			

DOUGLAS C-47 DAKOTA FREIGHTERS.

SE-BAZ	Esbjörn Viking		SE-BBR	Rörek Viking
SE-BBP	Torgny Viking			

AER LINGUS FLEET.

AIRSPEED CONSULS.

EI-ADB	Unnamed		EI-ADC	Unnamed

DOUGLAS DC-3 DAKOTAS.

EI-ACD	Unnamed		EI-ACL	St. Declan
EI-ACE	St. Colmcille		EI-ACM	St. Fintan
EI-ACF	St. Kieran		EI-ACT	St. Colman
EI-ACG	St. Malachy		EI-ADW	Unnamed
EI-ACH	Unnamed		EI-ADX	Unnamed
EI-ACI	St. Aidan		EI-ADY	Unnamed
EI-ACK	St. Albert			

AIR FRANCE FLEET

DOUGLAS DC-4 SKYMASTERS.

F-BBDA	Ciel de Bretagne	F-BBDI	Ciel de Provence
F-BBDB	Ciel de Touraine	F-BBDJ	Ciel Ile de France
F-BBDD	Ciel de Bourgogne	F-BBDK	Ciel de Normandie
F-BBDE	Ciel de Picardie	F-BBDL	Ciel d'Alsace
F-BBDF	Ciel d'Artois	F-BBDM	Ciel de Gascogne
F-BBDG	Ciel de Champagne	F-BBDN	Ciel de Lorraine
F-BBDH	Ciel de Bearn	F-BBDO	Ciel de Savoie

DOUGLAS C-54A SKYMASTER FREIGHTERS.

F-BELC	F-BELD	F-BELE	F-BELF

LOCKHEED CONSTELLATIONS.

F-BAZA	F-BAZI	F-BAZL	F-BAZO
F-BAZB	F-BAZJ	F-BAZM	F-BAZP
F-BAZC	F-BAZK	F-BAZN	F-BAZQ
F-BAZD			

LANGUEDOC 161s.

F-BATB	F-BATO	F-BATU	F-BCUG
F-BATC	F-BATP	F-BATV	F-BCUH
F-BATD	F-BATQ	F-BATX	F-BCUI
F-BATE	F-BATR	F-BATZ	F-BCUJ
F-BATG	F-BATS	F-BCUA	F-BCUK
F-BATI	F-BATT	F-BCUB	F-BCUL
F-BATJ	F-BCUK	F-BCUE	F-BCUM
F-BATN	F-BCUL	F-BCUF	F-BCUO

DOUGLAS DC-3 DAKOTAS.

F-BAIE	F-BAOE	F-BAXK	F-BCYQ
F-BAIF	F-BAXA	F-BAXL	F-BCYR
F-BAIG	F-BAXB	F-BAXM	F-BCYS
F-BAIH	F-BAXE	F-BAXP	F-BCYT
F-BAII	F-BAXF	F-BAXR	F-BCYU
F-BAIJ	F-BAXG	F-BAXS	F-BCYV
F-BAOA	F-BAXH	F-BBBA	F-BCYX
F-BAOC	F-BAXI	F-BBBE	F-BEFM
F-BAOD	F-BAXJ	F-BCYP	F-BEFN

DE HAVILLAND DRAGON RAPIDES.

F-BEDX	F-BEDY	F-BEDZ

CONSOLIDATED CATALINA FLYING-BOATS.

F-BBCB	F-BBCC	F-BBCD

LATECOERE 631 FLYING-BOATS.

F-BANU	Guillaumet	F-BDRA	Unnamed

AIR INDIA INTERNATIONAL FLEET.

LOCKHEED CONSTELLATIONS.

VT-CQP	*Malabar Princess*		VT-CQS	*Mogul Princess*
VT-CQR	*Rajput Princess*			

ALITALIA FLEET.

AVRO LANCASTRIANS.

(On loan from B.O.A.C.)

I-DALR	*Borea*		I-AHCB	*Grecale*
I-AHBX	*Maestrale*		I-AHCD	*Scirocco*
I-AHBY	*Libeccio*			

S.I.A.I. MARCHETTI S.M. 95s.

I-DALJ	*Cristoforo Colombo*		I-DALN	*Sebastiano Caboto*
I-DALK	*Amerigo Vespucci*		I-DALO	*Ugolino Vivaldi*
I-DALL	*Marco Polo*			

AMERICAN OVERSEAS AIRLINES FLEET.

(On services to Great Britain)

DOUGLAS C-54E SKYMASTERS.

NC 90901	*Flagship Stockholm*		NC 90905	*Flagship Glasgow*
NC 90902	*Flagship London*		NC 90906	*Flagship Copenhagen*
NC 90903	*Flagship Oslo*			

DOUGLAS C-54G SKYMASTERS.

NC 90910	*Flagship Shannon*		NC 90913	*Flagship Amsterdam*
NC 90911	*Flagship Reykjavik*		NC 90915	*Flagship Gander*
NC 90912	*Flagship Prestwick*		NC 90909	*Flagship Keflavik*

LOCKHEED L-49 CONSTELLATIONS.

NC 90921	*Flagship Sweden*		NC 90925	*Flagship Americ*
NC 90922	*Flagship Denmark*		NC 90926	*Flagship Eire*
NC 90923	*Flagship Great Britain*		NC 90927	*Flagship Norway*
NC 90924	*Flagship Holland*			

BRITISH EUROPEAN AIRWAYS FLEET.

VICKERS VIKING 1Bs.

G-AHPL	*Verdant*		G-AHPS	*Verity*
G-AHPM	*Verderer*		G-AIVB	*Vernal*
G-AHPN	*Ventnor*		G-AIVC	*Vernon*
G-AHPO	*Venture*		G-AIVD	*Veteran*
G-AHPP	*Venus*		G-AIVF	*Vibrant*
G-AHPR	*Verily*		G-AIVG	*Viceroy*

BRITISH EUROPEAN AIRWAYS—Contd.

G-AIVH	Vicinity	G-AJBO	Vintage
G-AIVI	Victor	G-AJBP	Vintner
G-AIVJ	Victoria	G-AJBS	Virgo
G-AIVK	Victory	G-AJBT	Viper
G-AIVL	Vigilant	G-AJBU	Virtue
G-AIVM	Vigorous	G-AJBV	Viscount
G-AIVN	Violet	G-AJBW	Vista
G-AIVO	Villian	G-AJBX	Vital
G-AJBM	Vincent	G-AJBY	Vitality
G-AJBN	Vindictive	G-AJCE	Vivacious

VICKERS VIKING IA (CREW TRAINING).

G-AHOY	Vanity

DOUGLAS DC-3 DAKOTAS.

G-AGHJ	G-AGIW	G-AHCT	G-AJHY
G-AGHL	G-AGIX	G-AHCU	G-AJHZ
G-AGHS	G-AGJZ	G-AHCV	G-AJIA
G-AGIP	G-AGYX	G-AHCW	G-AJIB
G-AGIS	G-AGZB	G-AHCX	G-AJIC
G-AGIU	G-AGZD	G-AHCY	

DOUGLAS DC-3 DAKOTA FREIGHTERS.

G-AGJV	G-AGJW	G-AGYZ	G-AHCZ

DE HAVILLAND DRAGON RAPIDES.

G-AFEZ	G-AGSK	G-AHKS	G-AHXV
G-AFRK	G-AGUP	G-AHKT	G-AHXW
G-AGJG	G-AGUR	G-AHKU	G-AHXX
G-AGPH	G-AGUU	G-AHKV	G-AHXY
G-AGSH	G-AGUV	G-AHLL	G-AHXZ

B.E.A. EXPERIMENTAL HELICOPTER UNIT.

Bell 47B	G-AKFA	Sikorsky S.51	G-AJOR
Bell 47B	G-AKFB	Sikorsky S.51	G-AJOV
Sikorsky S.51	G-AKCU		

BRITISH OVERSEAS AIRWAYS FLEET

LOCKHEED CONSTELLATIONS.

G-AHEJ	Bristol II	G-AHEM	Balmoral
G-AHEK	Berwick II	G-AHEN	Baltimore
G-AHEL	Bangor II	G-AKCE	Belfast

AVRO LANCASTRIAN FREIGHTERS.

G-AGLS	Nelson	G-AGMG	Nicosia
G-AGLT	Newcastle	G-AGMJ	Naseby
G-AGLW	Northampton	G-AGMK	Newbury
G-AGLY	Norfolk	G-AGMM	Nepal
G-AGMA	Newport	G-AKPY	Not yet named
G-AGMB	Norwich	G-AKPZ	Not yet named
G-AGME	Newhaven	G-AKRB	Not yet named

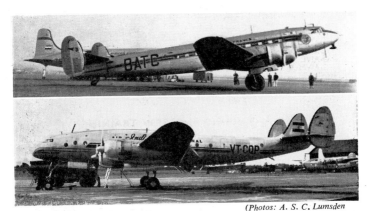

(Photos: A. S. C. Lumsden

Upper: Latest type of airliner in service with Air France, the Languedoc 161. Illustrated is F-BATC, a familiar London Airport visitor.
Lower: Air India International Constellation *Malabar Princess* at London Airport on arrival from Bombay.

(Photos: A. S. C. Lumsden

Upper: S.I.A.I. Marchetti S.M. 95 airliner of the Italian company Alitalia, five of which operate between Northolt and Rome.
Lower: D.H. Rapide of British European Airways. B.E.A. Rapides operate mainly on the Scottish island services.

British European Airways operate over 30 Vickers Viking IB airliners on European routes. With the familiar red "Speed-Key" insignia on nose and fin, G-AJBT *Viper* is illustrated. All B.E.A. Vikings have names beginning with "V"

Douglas Dakota G-AGJV of B.E.A. at Northolt.

(*Photos: A. S. C. Lumsden*

Avro Lancastrian, now employed as freighter by B.O.A.C. to Johannesburg and Sydney.

AVRO YORKS.

G-AGJA	Mildenhall	G-AGNX	Moray
G-AGJB	Marathon	G-AGNY	Melrose
G-AGJC	Malmesbury	G-AGNZ	Monmouth
G-AGJD	Mansfield	G-AGOA	Montrose
G-AGJE	Middlesex	G-AGOB	Milford
G-AGNL	Mersey	G-AGOC	Malta
G-AGNM	Murchison	G-AGOD	Midlothian
G-AGNN	Madras	G-AGOE	Medway
G-AGNO	Manton	G-AGOF	Macduff
G-AGNP	Manchester	G-AGSL	Morley
G-AGNS	Melville	G-AGSM	Malvern
G-AGNT	Mandalay	G-AGSN	Marlow
G-AGNU	Montgomery	G-AGSO	Marston
G-AGNV	Morville	G-AGSP	Malborough
G-AGNW	Morecambe		

CONSOLIDATED LIBERATOR II FREIGHTERS.

G-AGJP	G-AHYD	G-AHYF
G-AHYB	G-AHYE	G-AHYG

DOUGLAS DC-3 DAKOTAS.

G-AGGA	G-AGKA	G-AGKJ	G-AGND
G-AGHE	G-AGKB	G-AGKK	G-AGNE
G-AGHF	G-AGKC	G-AGKL	G-AGNF
G-AGHH	G-AGKE	G-AGKN	G-AGNG
G-AGHM	G-AGKF	G-AGMZ	G-AGNK
G-AGHN	G-ACKG	G-AGNB	G-AGZC
G-AGHO	G-AGKH	G-AGNC	G-AGZE
G-AGIZ	G-AGKI		

SHORT S.45 SOLENT FLYING-BOATS.

G-AHIL	Salisbury	G-AHIT	Severn
G-AHIM	Scarborough	G-AHIU	Solway
G-AHIN	Southampton	G-AHIV	Salcombe
G-AHIO	Somerset	G-AHIW	Stornoway
G-AHIR	Sark	G-AHIX	Sussex
G-AHIS	Scapa	G-AHIY	Southsea

SHORT S.25 SANDRINGHAM VII FLYING-BOATS.

G-AKCO	St. George	G-AKCR	Not yet named
G-AKCP	St. David		

SHORT S.25 SANDRINGHAM V (" PLYMOUTH CLASS ") FLYING-BOATS.

G-AHYY	Portsmouth	G-AHZE	Portsea
G-AHZA	Penzance	G-AHZF	Poole
G-AHZC	Pembroke	G-AHZG	Pevensey
G-AHZD	Portmarnock	G-AJMZ	Perth

SHORT S.25 SUNDERLAND III (" HYTHE CLASS ") FLYING-BOATS.

G-AGER	Hadfield	G-AGHZ	Hawkesbury
G-AGEU	Hampshire	G-AGIA	Haslemere
G-AGEW	Hanwell	G-AGJJ	Henley
G-AGHX	Harlequin	G-AGJK	Howard

G-AGJL	*Hobart*	G-AGKW	*Hotspur*
G-AGJM	*Hythe*	G-AGKX	*Himalaya*
G-AGJN	*Hudson*	G-AGKY	*Hungerford*
G-AGJO	*Honduras*	G-AGKZ	*Harwich*
G-AGKV	*Huntingdon*	G-AGLA	*Hunter*

BOEING STRATOCRUISERS.

The following registration letters have been announced as reserved for use on the B.O.A.C. Stratocruisers now building in the U.S.A., but it is to be noted that these are provisional and liable to alteration. No names have yet been decided for these aircraft which are to come into service on B.O.A.C.'s Atlantic route during 1949.

G-AKGH	G-AKGJ	G-AKGM
G-AKGI	G-AKGK	

BRITISH SOUTH AMERICAN AIRWAYS FLEET.

AVRO TUDOR IVs.

G-AHNJ	*Star Panther*	G-AHNN	*Star Leopard*
G-AHNK	*Star Lion*		

AVRO YORK IGs.

G-AHEX	*Star Venture*	G-AHFD	*Star Mist*
G-AHEY	*Star Quest*	G-AHFE	*Star Vista*
G-AHFA	*Star Dale*	G-AHFF	*Star Gleam*
G-AHFB	*Star Stream*	G-AHFG	*Star Haze*
G-AHFC	*Star Dew*	G-AHFH	*Star Glitter*

AVRO LANCASTRIAN IIs.

G-AKFF	*Star Flight*	G-AKTB	*Star Glory*
G-AKFG	*Star Traveller*	G-AKTC	*Star Fortune*
G-AKMW	*Star Bright*	G-AKTG	*Star Crest*

AVRO LANCASTRIAN IIIs.

G-AGWI	*Star Land*	G-AGWL	*Star Guide*

AVRO LANCASTER FREIGHTERS.

G-AGUJ	*Star Pilot*	G-AGUM	*Star Ward*

AIRSPEED OXFORD.

G-AIVY	*Star Mentor*

CENTRAL AFRICAN AIRWAYS FLEET.

(Operating on special flights into Great Britain).

VICKERS VIKINGS.

VP-YEW	VP-YEY	VP-YHT
VP-YEX	VP-YHJ	

CIE AIR TRANSPORT FLEET.

(Operating into Great Britain).

BEECH 18 EXPEDITERS.

		BRISTOL 170s.	
F-BEDB	F-BEDD	F-BEND	F-BENH
F-BEDC	F-BEDE	F-BENF	

COBETA FLEET.

(Operated by Cobeta and owned by John Mahieu Aviation of Brussels).

DOUGLAS DC-3 DAKOTA.

OO-APC

LOCKHEED HUDSON.

OO-API

C.S.A. FLEET.

(On services to Great Britain).

DOUGLAS DC-3 DAKOTAS.

OK-WAA	OK-WDC	OK-WDL	OK-WDU
OK-WCN	OK-WDE	OK-WDN	OK-WDV
OK-WCO	OK-WDF	OK-WDO	OK-WDW
OK-WCP	OK-WDG	OK-WDP	OK-WDY
OK-WCR	OK-WDH	OK-WDQ	OK-WDZ
OK-WCS	OK-WDI	OK-WDR	OK-XDH
OK-WCT	OK-WDJ	OK-WDS	OK-XDN
OK-WDA	OK-WDK	OK-WDT	

D.D.L. FLEET.

(Component of Scandinavian Airways System).

DOUGLAS DC-6s.

	DOUGLAS DC-4 SKYMASTERS.	
OY-AAE	OY-DFI	Dan Viking
OY-AAF	OY-DFO	Rolf Viking

VICKERS VIKINGS.

OY-DLA	Tor Viking	OY-DLO	Tormund Viking
OY-DLE	Torleif Viking	OY-DLU	Torlak Viking

DOUGLAS DC-3 DAKOTAS.

OY-DCA	Arv Viking	OY-DDA	Sven Viking
OY-DCE	Gorm Viking	OY-DDE	Erik Viking
OY-DCO	Orm Viking	OY-DDI	Roar Viking
OY-DCU	Ulf Viking	OY-DDY	Trym Viking
OY-DCY	Sten Viking		

DOUGLAS C-47 DAKOTA FREIGHTERS.

OY-AAB	Regnar Viking	OY-AYB	Bjorn Viking
OY-AOB	Bjarke Viking	OY-DDO	Odd Viking
OY-AUB	Bjarne Viking	OY-DDU	Leif Viking

JUNKERS JU 52 FREIGHTER.

OY-DFU   Uffe Viking

D.N.L. FLEET.

(Component of Scandinavian Airways System).

DOUGLAS DC-6s.

| LN-LAG | Sverre Viking | | LN-LAH | Harald Viking |

DOUGLAS DC-4 SKYMASTERS.

| LN-IAD | Haakon Viking | | LN-IAE | Olav Viking |

DOUGLAS DC-3 DAKOTAS.

LN-IAF	Nordfugl		LN-IAN	Nordvind
LN-IAG	Nordegg		LN-IAO	Nordodd
LN-IAH	Nordheim		LN-IAP	Nordpol
LN-IAI	Nordis		LN-IAR	Nordkapp
LN-IAK	Nordkyn		LN-IAS	Nordpil
LN-IAL	Nordlys		LN-IAT	Nordtind
LN-IAM	Nordvard			

SHORT SANDRINGHAM VI FLYING-BOATS.

LN-IAU	Bamse Brakar		LN-LAI	Jutulen
LN-IAW	Bukken Bruse			

F.A.M.A. FLEET.

(Note.: " G.B." indicates aircraft used most on routes to Great Britain).

AVRO YORKS.

LV-AFV (G.B.)	LV-AFZ (G.B.)
LV-AFY (G.B.)	

AVRO LANCASTRIANS.

| LV-ACU (G.B.) | LV-ACV (G.B.) |

DOUGLAS DC-4B SKYMASTERS.

LV-ABP (G.B.)		LV-AEU (G.B.)
LV-ABS (G.B.)		LV-AFD (G.B.)

DOUGLAS DC-4A SKYMASTERS.

LV-ABI	LV-ABO
LV-ABM	LV-ABR
LV-ABN	LV-ADH

VICKERS VIKINGS.

LV-AEW		LV-AFL		LV-AFI
LV-AEV		LV-AFF		LV-AFU

HELLENIC AIRLINES FLEET.

CONSOLIDATED LIBERATOR.

| SX-DAA | Maid of Athens |

DOUGLAS DC-3 DAKOTAS.

SX-BBA		SX-BBC
SX-BBB		SX-BBD

IBERIA FLEET.

DOUGLAS DC-2s.

EC-AAA	¡EC-AAD
EC-AAB	

DOUGLAS DC-4 SKYMASTERS.

EC-ACD	EC-ACF
EC-ACE	

D.H. DRAGON RAPIDES.

EC-AAV	EC-BAC
EC-AAS	EC-BAG

DOUGLAS DC-3 DAKOTAS.

EC-ABC	EC-ABQ
EC-ABK	EC-ACG
EC-ABL	EC-ACH
EC-ABM	EC-ACI
EC-ABP	EC-ACX
EC-ABN	

JUNKERS JU 52/3ms.

EC-AAH	EC-AAU
EC-AAI	EC-ABS¡
EC-AAK	EC-ABR
EC-AAL	

IRAQI AIRWAYS FLEET.

(Operating into Great Britain).

VICKERS VIKINGS.

YI-ABP	YI-ABQ	YI-ABR

K.L.M. FLEET.

LOCKHEED L-49 CONSTELLATIONS.

PH-TAU	Utrecht	PH-TDA	Arnhem
PH-TAV	Venlo	PH-TEN	Nijmegen
PH-TAW	Walcheren	PH-TEO	Overloon

LOCKHEED L-749 CONSTELLATIONS.

PH-TDB	Batavia	PH-TDH	Holland
PH-TDC	Curacao	PH-TEP	Pontianak
PH-TDD	Delft	PH-TER	Roermond
PH-TDE	Eindhoven	PH-TES	Soerabaja
PH-TDF	Franeker	PH-TET	Tilburg
PH-TDG	Gouda		

DOUGLAS DC-6s.

PH-TPB	Prins Bernhard	PH-TPM	Prinses Marijke
PH-TPI	Prinses Irene	PH-TPP	Prinses Margriet
PH-TPJ	Prinses Juliana	PH-TPT	Prinses Beatrix

DOUGLAS DC-4 SKYMASTERS.

PH-TAP	Paramaribo	PJ-TAR	Rotterdam
PH-TCE	Edam	PJ-TAS	Schiedam
PH-TCF	Friesland	PJ-TAT	Twenthe

DOUGLAS C-54 SKYMASTERS.

(Note.—" F " indicates freighters).

PH-TAH	PH-TEY (F)	PH-TLO
PH-TAM	PH-TEZ (F)	PH-TLW
PH-TBU	PH-TLK	PH-TSC

DOUGLAS DC-3 [DAKOTAS.

(Note.—" F " indicates freighter ; " P " photographic aircraft ;
" T " trainer and freighter).

PH-TAY	PH-TBM (P)	PH-TCK (T)	PH-TDU
PH-TAZ	PH-TBP	PH-TCL	PH-TDV
PH-TBG	PH-TBV	PH-TCS	PH-TDW
PH-TBI	PH-TBX	PH-TCT	PH-TDZ
PH-TBK (T)	PH-TBY	PH-TCU	PH-TEU
PH-TBH (T)	PH-TBZ	PH-TDS	PH-TEW (T)
PH-TBL	PH-TCI	PH-TDT	

(Dakotas in West Indies Division).

PJ-ALA	*Ala Blanca*	PJ-ALE (F)	PJ-ALI (P)
PJ-ALB	*Blauwduif*	PJ-ALG (P)	PJ-ALP
PJ-ALC	*Chuchubi*	PJ-ALH (P)	
PJ-ALD	*Dekla*		

CONVAIR 240 LINERS.

These aircraft are to replace Dakotas on many European routes of
K.L.M. and are to commence delivery from the U.S.A. in the summer.
Deliveries are expected to be completed before the end of 1948.   K.L.M.
announces that the Convairs will be named after Dutch painters.

PH-TEA	PH-TED	PH-TEG	PH-TEK
PH-TEB	PH-TEE	PH-TEH	PH-TEL
PH-TEC	PH-TEF	PH-TEI	PH-TEM

LUXEMBOURG AIRLINES FLEET.

DOUGLAS DC-3 DAKOTAS.

LX-LAA   LX-LAB

PAN AMERICAN WORLD AIRWAYS FLEET.

(Atlantic Division).

LOCKHEED L-49 CONSTELLATIONS.

NC 88832	*Clipper Flora Temple*	NC 88856	*Clipper Paul Jones*
NC 88833	*Clipper Bald Eagle*	NC 88857	*Clipper Flying Mist*
NC 88836	*Clipper Mayflower*	NC 88859	*Clipper Flying Eagle*
NC 88837	*Clipper Challenger*	NC 88861	*Clipper Winged Arrow*
NC 88838	*Clipper Donald McKay*	NC 88865	*Clipper White Falcon*
NC 88846	*Clipper Great Republic*	NC 88868	*Clipper Golden Fleece*
NC 88847	*Clipper Hotspur*	NC 86527	*Clipper Glory of the Skies*
NC 88850	*Clipper Intrepid*	NC 86529	*Clipper Romance of the Skies*
NC 88855	*Clipper Invincible*	NC 86530	*Clipper America*

DOUGLAS DC-4 SKYMASTERS.

NC 88919	*Clipper Panama*	NC 88945	*Clipper Gladiator*
NC 88927	*Clipper Skylark*		

DOUGLAS DC-3 DAKOTAS.

NC 54227	*Clipper Pan American*	NC 79009	*Clipper Undaunted*
NC 79008	*Clipper Robin Hood*	NC 79010	*Clipper Live Yankee*

PANAIR DO BRASIL FLEET.

(Operating into Great Britain).
LOCKHEED CONSTELLATIONS.*

PP-PCB	PP-PCG	PP-PDA
PP-PCF	PP-PCR	

Q.E.A. FLEET.

(Operating into Great Britain).
LOCKHEED CONSTELLATIONS.

VH-EAA	Ross Smith	VH-EAC	Harry Hawker
VH-EAB	Lawrence Hargrave	VH-EAD	Chas. Kingsford Smith

SOUTH AFRICAN AIRWAYS FLEET.

(On services to Great Britain).
DOUGLAS DC-4 SKYMASTERS.

ZS-AUA	Tafelberg	ZS-BMH	Lebombo
ZS-AUG	Drakensberg	ZS-BWN	Swartberg
ZS-BMF	Amatola	L5-AU3	Outeniqua
ZS-BMG	Magaliesberg		

S.A.B.E.N.A. FLEET.

DOUGLAS DC-6s.

OO-AWA	OO-AWC
OO-AWB	

DOUGLAS DC-4 SKYMASTERS.

OO-CBI	OO-CBN
OO-CBJ	OO-CBO
OO-CBK	OO-CBP
OO-CBL	OO-CBQ
OO-CBM	

DOUGLAS DC-3 DAKOTAS.

OO-AUL	OO-AUV
OO-AUM	OO-AUX
OO-AUN	OO-AUY
OO-AUO	OO-AUZ
OO-AUP	OO-AWF
OO-AUQ	OO-AWG
OO-AUR	OO-AWK
OO-AUS	OO-AWN
OO-AUT	

D.H. DOVES.

OO-AWD	OO-AWE

SWISSAIR FLEET.

DOUGLAS DC-4 SKYMASTERS.

HB-ILA	HB-ILI
HB-ILE	HB-ILO

DOUGLAS DC-2s.

HB-ITE	HB-ITO

DOUGLAS DC-3 DAKOTAS.

HB-IRA	HB-IRI
HB-IRB	HB-IRK
HB-IRD	HB-IRL
HB-IRE	HB-IRM
HB-IRF	HB-IRN
HB-IRG	HB-IRO
	HB-IRX

CONVAIR 240 LINERS.†

HB-IRP	HB-IRS
HB-IRR	HB-IRT

* Panair do Brazil Constellations are known to the company as the [Bandeirante or "Pioneer" Class.
† On order from U.S.A., delivery expected before the end of 1948.

TRANS-CANADA AIRLINES FLEET.

(Operating into Great Britain).

CANADAIR DC-4M-2 NORTH STARS.

CF-TFA	CF-TFF	CF-TFK	CF-TFP
CF-TFB	CF-TFG	CF-TFL	CF-TFQ
CF-TFC	CF-TFH	CF-TFM	CF-TFR
CF-TFD	CF-TFI	CF-TFN	CF-TFS
CF-TFE	CF-TFJ	CF-TFO	CF-TFT

CANADAIR DC-4M-1 NORTH STARS.*

CF-TEK	CF-TEM	CF-TEP
CF-TEL	CF-TEO	CF-TEQ

TRANS-WORLD AIRLINE FLEET.

(Operating through Shannon).

LOCKHEED L-49 CONSTELLATIONS.

NC 86506	Star of Dublin	NC 90814	Star of Cairo
NC 86511	Star of Paris	NC 90815	Star of Lisbon
NC 86536	Star of Rome	NC 90816	Star of Geneva

LOCKHEED L-749 CONSTELLATIONS.

NC 91201	Star of New York	NC 91207	Star of Missouri
NC 91202	Star of Pennsylvania	NC 91208	Star of Massachusetts
NC 91203	Star of Ohio	NC 91209	Star of New Mexico
NC 91204	Star of Indiana	NC 91210	Star of Delaware
NC 91205	Star of Michigan	NC 91211	Star of Arizona
NC 91206	Star of Illinois	NC 91212	Star of California

DOUGLAS C-54B SKYMASTERS.

NC 34538	The Shalimar	NC 44994	The Alhambra
NC 34537	The Citadel	NC 86571	The Gates of Suez
NC 34577	The Moulein Pagoda		

DOUGLAS C-54E SKYMASTERS.

NC 45341	The Taj Mahal	NC 45344	The Colosseum
NC 45342	The Shamrock	NC 45345	The Arc de Triomphe
NC 45343	The Sphinx	NC 45346	The Acropolis

DOUGLAS C-54G SKYMASTERS.

NC 14747	The Bombay Merchant	NC 79067	The Shanghai Merchant
NC 79066	Unnamed		

* On loan from R.C.A.F., to be returned shortly.

Many charter companies are now operating their aircraft on regular scheduled internal airlines, details of which will be found on another page. To comply with the terms of the Civil Aviation Act, such companies are operating as associates of British European Airways.

Charter aircraft included in this list are either operating such internal services or are available for long-distance charter and freight work. Light aircraft, and aircraft available merely for local and pleasure flights have been excluded, and these can be found in the companion book "A.B.C. OF BRITISH AIRCRAFT MARKINGS."

AIR CHARTER LTD. FLEET.
(Aircraft based at Croydon and Bovingdon).

AIRSPEED CONSUL.
G-AJGH

D.H. DRAGON RAPIDES.
G-AFHY | G-AJFU

AIR CONTRACTORS LTD. FLEET.
(Aircraft based at Bovingdon).

DOUGLAS DAKOTAS.
G-AIWC	G-AIWE
G-AIWD	

AIR ENTERPRISES LTD. FLEET.
(Aircraft based at Croydon and Gatwick).

AIRSPEED CONSUL.
G-AJLJ

D.H. DRAGON RAPIDES.
G-AFMJ	G-AKOA
G-AKNX	G-AKOB
G-AKNY	G-AKRS
G-AKNZ	

AIR NAVIGATION AND TRADING CO. LTD. FLEET.
(Aircraft based at Squire's Gate).

D.H. DRAGON RAPIDES.
G-AKOY	G-AKZT
G-AKSG	

SUPERMARINE SEA OTTERS.
G-AKRG | G-AKYH

AIR TRANSPORT (CHARTER) (C.I.) LTD. FLEET.
(Aircraft based at Jersey).

DOUGLAS DAKOTAS.
G-AJBH	G-AKIL
G-AJBG	

D.H. DRAGON RAPIDES.
G-AFFB	G-AIUL
G-AGWC	

AIRWORK LTD. FLEET.
(Aircraft based at Blackbushe).

BRISTOL FREIGHTER.
G-AHJD

VICKERS VIKINGS.
G-AIXR	G-AJFR
G-AIXS	G-AJFS
G-AJFP	G-AJFT

(Aircraft based at Gatwick).

AIRSPEED CONSUL.
G-AIKR

BIRKETT AIR SERVICES LTD. FLEET.
(Aircraft based at Croydon).

AIRSPEED CONSUL.
G-AJLK

D.H. DRAGON RAPIDES.
G-AJBJ   G-AJDN

BLUE LINE AIRWAYS LTD. FLEET.

(Aircraft based at Tollerton, Nottingham).

AVRO ANSONS.

G-AJFX	G-AKFL
G-AKFK	G-AKFM

BRITISH AIR TRANSPORT LTD. FLEET.

(Aircraft based at Croydon and Redhill, Surrey).

AIRSPEED CONSULS.

G-AHEH	G-AIDZ
G-AHFS	G-AIEA
G-AIDY	

AVRO ANSONS.

G-AHKH	G-AIWV
G-AIWW	G-AIXU

D.H. FLAMINGO.
G-AFYH

A number of Flamingo aircraft are being reconditioned and will appear in service shortly. These aircraft are listed below :—

G-AFYF	G-AFYK
G-AFYJ	G-AFYL

BRITISH AVIATION SERVICES LTD. FLEET.

(Including Silver City Airways, Ltd.).

(Aircraft based at Blackbushe).

AIRSPEED CONSULS.

G-AHRK	G-AIBF

AVRO LANCASTRIAN.
G-AHBV

D.H. DOVES.

G-AIWF	G-AKJP
G-AKJG	

BRISTOL FREIGHTER.
G-AGVC

BRISTOL WAYFARER.
G-AHJC

LOCKHEED LODESTAR.
G-AJAW

DOUGLAS DAKOTAS.

G-AJAV	G-AIRH

BRITISH NEDERLAND AIR SERVICES LTD. FLEET.

(Aircraft based at Bovingdon).

DOUGLAS DAKOTAS.

G-AJZD	G-AJZX

MILES AEROVAN IV.
G-AISI

BROOKLANDS AVIATION LTD. FLEET.

(Aircraft based at Sywell, Northants and Shoreham, Sussex).

D.H. DRAGON RAPIDES.

G-AJHO	G-AJHP

CAMBRIAN AIR SERVICES FLEET.

(Aircraft based at Cardiff Airport).

D.H. DRAGON RAPIDES.

G-AGZJ	G-AKUC
G-AKUB	

CHARTAIR LTD. FLEET.

(Aircraft based at Croydon Airport).

AIRSPEED CONSULS.

G-AIKO	G-AIUR
G-AIKX	G-AIUX
G-AIOM	G-AJGG

CIRO AVIATION FLEET.

(Aircraft based at Gatwick Airport).

D.H. DRAGON RAPIDES.

G-AFMA	G-AKGV

DOUGLAS DAKOTAS.

G-AIJD	ZS-BYX
G-AKJN	

CULLIFORD AIRLINES LTD. FLEET.

(Aircraft based at Squire's Gate).

AVRO ANSON.
G-AIXO

MILES AEROVAN.
G-AJZG

DENNIS AVIATION LTD. FLEET.

(Aircraft based at Croydon and Gatwick).

AIRSPEED CONSULS.

G-AHMB	G-AIOR

HORNTON AIRWAYS LTD. FLEET.

(Aircraft based at Heston).

AIRSPEED CONSULS.

G-AIOP	G-AIUW
G-AIUV	

D.H. DRAGON RAPIDE.

G-AIUO

DOUGLAS DAKOTA.

G-AKLL

HUNTING AIR TRAVEL LTD. FLEET.

(Aircraft based at Croydon and Gatwick).

D.H. DOVES.

G-AJBI	G-AJDP

D.H. DRAGON RAPIDES.

G-AHPU	G-AHWF

VICKERS VIKINGS.

G-AHPI	G-AHPJ

INTERNATIONAL AIRWAYS LTD. FLEET.

(Aircraft based at Croydon Airport).

AIRSPEED CONSULS.

G-AHXP	G-AIUU
G-AIIS	G-AJGB
G-AIOL	

AVRO ANSONS.

G-AGUH	G-AITI

ISLAND AIR CHARTERS LTD. FLEET.

(Aircraft based at Jersey).

D.H. DRAGON RAPIDES.

G-AHPT	G-AJFK

ISLAND AIR SERVICES LTD. FLEET.

(Aircraft based at St. Mary's, Scilly Isles and Croydon).

D.H. DRAGON RAPIDES.

G-AGSJ	G-AIOY

KEARSLEY AIRWAYS LTD. FLEET.

(Aircraft based at Stansted Airport).

DOUGLAS DAKOTAS.

G-AKAR	G-AKOZ
G-AKDT	

LANCASHIRE AIRCRAFT CORPORATION FLEET.

(Aircraft based at Squire's Gate, Blackpool ; Yeadon, Leeds and Bovingdon, Herts).

AIRSPEED CONSULS.

G-AHMD	G-AHZW
G-AHZV	

D.H. DRAGON RAPIDES.

G-AHEA	G-AJKY
G-AJKW	G-AKNV
G-AJKX	G-AKNW

HANDLEY PAGE HALIFAXES.

G-AIHV	Air Trader
G-AIHX	Air Explorer
G-AIHY	Unnamed
G-AJZY	Air Monarch
G-AJZZ	Air Viceroy
G-AKEC	Air Voyager

L.A.M.S. LTD. FLEET.

(Aircraft based at Stansted Airport).

HANDLEY PAGE HALIFAX FREIGHTERS.

G-AHZK	G-AIWJ
G-AHZL	G-AIWK
G-AHZO	G-AIWP

MANX AIR CHARTERS LTD. FLEET.

(Aircraft based at Ronaldsway, Isle of Man).

D.H. DRAGON RAPIDES.

G-AJGV	G-AKIF
G-AKGY	G-AKSE

MORTON AIR SERVICES LTD. FLEET.

(Aircraft based at Croydon Airport and Speke, Liverpool).

AIRSPEED CONSULS.

G-AHFT	G-AIOS
G-AHJX	G-AIOU
G-AIAH	G-AIOW

D.H. DOVES.

G-AKST	G-AKSU

D.H. DRAGON RAPIDES.

G-AGWP	G-AHIA
G-AGWR	G-AKUS

NEWMAN AIRWAYS FLEET.

(Aircraft based at Croydon Airport).

D.H. DRAGON RAPIDE.

G-AKPA

NORTHERN AIR CHARTER LTD. FLEET.

(Aircraft based at Woolsington, Newcastle-on-Tyne and Greatham, West Hartlepool).

AIRSPEED CONSULS.

G-AJGA	G-AJLH

D.H. DRAGON RAPIDE.

G-AKNN

NORTH SEA AIR TRANSPORT FLEET.

(Aircraft based at Hanworth, Feltham, Middlesex).

AVRO ANSON.

G-AIRX

D.H. DRAGON RAPIDES.

G-AHAG	G-AHTY
G-AHGD	G-AIWG
G-AHLU	G-AIWZ

LOCKHEED 12A.

G-AGDT

LOCKHEED 14.

G-AGBG

OLLEY AIR SERVICE LTD. FLEET.

(Aircraft based at Croydon Airport).

AIRSPEED CONSULS.

G-AIUY	G-AJLR
G-AJGD	

D.H. DOVES.

G-AJOT	G-AKSK
G-AKJR	

D.H. DRAGON RAPIDES.

G-AGSI	G-AKSB
G-AHGG	G-AKSD
G-AIYE	

PATRICK-DUVAL AVIATION SERVICES FLEET.

(Aircraft based at Elmdon Airport, Birmingham).

AIRSPEED CONSULS.

G-AIOT	G-AIOV

MILES AEROVANS.

G-AJKP	G-AJOF

SCOTTISH AIRLINES FLEET.

(Aircraft based at Prestwick Airport).

AIRSPEED OXFORD.

G-AHDZ

CONSOLIDATED LIBERATORS

G-AHDY	G-AHZP
G-AHZH	G-AHZR

DOUGLAS DC-3 DAKOTAS.

G-AGWS	G-AGZG
G-AGZF	G-AJVY

FOKKER F.22.

G-AFZP

SIVEWRIGHT AIRWAYS LTD. FLEET.

(Aircraft based at Barton Airport and Ringway Airport, Manchester).

AVRO XIX ANSONS.

G-AHXK	G-AHYN

D.H. DRAGON RAPIDES.

G-AJMY	G-AKMG

DOUGLAS DC-3 DAKOTAS.

G-AKAY	G-AKSM

SKYWAYS LTD. FLEET.
(Aircraft based at Dunsfold, Surrey).

AVRO LANCASTRIANS.
G-AGLV	Sky Lane
G-AHBT	Sky Ranger
G-AHBZ	Sky Ambassador
G-AHCC	Sky Chieftain
G-AJPP	Sky Consort

AVRO LANCASTER FREIGHTERS.
G-AKAB	Sky Trainer

AVRO YORKS.
G-AHFI	Sky Way
G-AHLV	Sky Courier

D.H. DOVE.
G-AHRB	Sky Maid

DOUGLAS DC-3 DAKOTAS.
G-AGBD	Sky Hawk
G-AICV	Sky Liner

DOUGLAS DC-4 SKYMASTERS.
G-AJPL	Sky Wisdom
G-AJPO	Sky Alliance
G-AJPM	Sky Freedom
G-AJPN	Sky Champion

D.H. DRAGON RAPIDE.
G-AHFJ	Sky Trail

LOCKHEED 12A.
G-AGWN	Unnamed

SOUTHERN AIRCRAFT (GATWICK) LTD. FLEET.
(Aircraft based at Gatwick Airport).

AVRO ANSON.
G-AKEW

D.H. DRAGON RAPIDES.
G-AJTU	G-AKOO

TRENT VALLEY AVIATION LTD. FLEET.
(Aircraft based at Tollerton, Nottingham).

DOUGLAS DC-3 DAKOTA.
G-AJPF

ULSTER AVIATION LTD. FLEET.
(Aircraft based at Newtownards Airport, Belfast).

AIRSPEED CONSUL.
G-AIKT

D.H. DRAGON RAPIDES.
G-AGIF	G-AHLN

MILES AEROVANS.
G-AJKU	G-AJTD

WESTERN AIRWAYS FLEET.
(Aircraft based at Weston-super-Mare).

AVRO ANSONS.
G-AIOB	G-AITJ
G-AITK	

WESTMINSTER AIRWAYS FLEET.
(Aircraft based at Blackbushe, Surrey and Croydon Airport).

AIRSPEED CONSULS.
G-AJLI	G-AJNG

DOUGLAS DC-3 DAKOTAS
G-AJAY	G-AJAZ

WORLD AIR FREIGHT FLEET.
(Aircraft based at Bovingdon).

HANDLEY PAGE HALIFAX FREIGHTERS.
G-AJNZ	G-AKGZ

ALPHABETICAL GUIDE TO AIR LINER REGISTRATIONS.

CF—CANADA.

CF-TEK	
CF-TEL	Canadair
CF-TEM	North Star I
CF-TEO	of Trans-Canada
CF-TEP	Air Lines
CF-TFA	
CF-TFB	
CF-TFC	
CF-TFD	
CF-TFE	
CF-TFF	
CF-TFG	
CF-TFH	
CF-TFI	Canadair
CF-TFJ	North Star II
CF-TFK	of Trans-Canada
CF-TFL	Air Lines
CF-TFM	
CF-TFN	
CF-TFO	
CF-TFP	
CF-TFR	
CF-TFS	
CF-TFT	

EC—SPAIN.

EC-AAA	Douglas DC-2
EC-AAB	of Iberia
EC-AAD	
EC-AAH	
EC-AAI	Junkers
EC-AAK	Ju 52/3m
EC-AAL	of Iberia
EC-AAU	
EC-AAV	D.H. Dragon
EC-AAS	Rapide of Iberia
EC-ABC	
EC-ABK	
EC-ABM	Douglas Dakota
EC-ABN	of Iberia
EC-ABP	
EC-ABQ	
EC-ACD	Douglas
EC-ACE	Skymaster
EC-ACF	of Iberia
EC-ACG	
EC-ACH	Douglas Dakota
EC-ACI	of Iberia
EC-ACX	
EC-BAC	D.H. Dragon
EC-BAG	Rapide of Iberia

EI—EIRE.

EI-ACD	
EI-ACE	
EI-ACF	
EI-ACG	
EI-ACH	Douglas Dakota
EI-ACI	of Aer Lingus
EI-ACK	
EI-ACL	
EI-ACM	
EI-ACT	
EI-ADB	Airspeed Consul
EI-ADC	of Aer Lingus
EI-ADW	
EI-ADX	Douglas Dakota
EI-ADY	of Aer Lingus

F—FRANCE.

F-BAIE	
F-BAIF	
F-BAIG	Douglas Dakota
F-BAIH	of Air France
F-BAII	
F-BAIJ	
F-BANU	Latecoere 631 of Air France
F-BAOA	
F-BAOC	Douglas Dakota
F-BAOD	of Air France
F-BAOE	
F-BATB	
F-BATC	
F-BATD	
F-BATE	
F-BATG	
F-BATI	
F-BATJ	
F-BATN	
F-BATO	Languedoc 161
F-BATP	of Air France
F-BATQ	
F-BATR	
F-BATS	
F-BATT	
F-BATU	
F-BATV	
F-BATX	
F-BATZ	
F-BAXA	
F-BAXB	
F-BAXE	
F-BAXF	
F-BAXG	
F-BAXH	
F-BAXI	Douglas Dakota
F-BAXJ	of Air France
F-BAXK	
F-BAXL	
F-BAXM	
F-BAXP	
F-BAXS	
F-BAZA	
F-BAZB	
F-BAZC	
F-BAZD	
F-BAZI	
F-BAZJ	
F-BAZK	Lockheed Constellation
F-BAZL	of Air France
F-BAZM	
F-BAZN	
F-BAZO	
F-BAZP	
F-BAZQ	
F-BBBA	Douglas Dakota
F-BBBE	of Air France
F-BBCB	Consolidated
F-BBCC	Catalina
F-BBCD	of Air France

F-BBDA	
F-BBDB	
F-BBDD	
F-BBDE	
F-BBDF	
F-BBDG	
F-BBDH	Douglas
F-BBDI	Skymaster
F-BBDJ	of Air France
F-BBDK	
F-BBDL	
F-BBDM	
F-BBDN	
F-BBDO	
F-BCUA	
F-BCUB	
F-BCUE	
F-BCUF	
F-BCUG	
F-BCUH	Languedoc 161
F-BCUI	of Air France
F-BCUJ	
F-BCUK	
F-BCUL	
F-BCUM	
F-BCUO	
F-BCYP	
F-BCYQ	
F-BCYR	
F-BCYS	Douglas Dakota
F-BCYT	of Air France
F-BCYU	
F-BCYV	
F-BCYX	
F-BDRA	Latecoere 631 of Air France
F-BEDB	Beech
F-BEDC	Expeditor
F-BEDD	of Air Transport
F-BEDE	
F-BEDX	D.H. Dragon
F-BEDY	Rapide
F-BEDZ	of Air France
F-BEFM	Douglas Dakota
F-BEFN	of Air France
F-BELC	Douglas
F-BELD	Skymaster
F-BELE	of Air France
P-BELF	
F-BEND	Bristol 170
F-BENF	of Air Transport
F-BENH	

G—GREAT BRITAIN

G-AFEZ	D.H. Dragon Rapide of British European Airways
G-AFFB	D.H. Dragon Rapide of Air Transport (Charter) (C.I.)
G-AFHY	D.H. Dragon Rapide of Air Charter Ltd.

26

Upper: A Consolidated Liberator freighter of B.O.A.C. as employed on the route to Montreal via Prestwick.

Lower: British Overseas Airways has six Lockheed Constellations on the Atlantic route and has recently purchased five more for the route to Australia. Here is *Berwick* G-AHEK.

(*Photos: A. S. C. Lumsden*)

Upper: Avro York G-AGOF *Macduff* of British Overseas Airways Corporation. B.O.A.C. Yorks fly to the Middle East, West Africa and Singapore.

Lower: One of the 30 Douglas Dakotas still in service with B.O.A.C. Dakotas operate the route from London Airport to Cairo.

Short Sandringham flying-boat G-AHYY *Portsmouth*, one of 10 "Plymouth" Class boats used by B.O.A.C. on the Dragon Route to the Far East and Japan, departing from Berth 50, Southampton.

(Photos: B.O.A.C.

Short Solent G-AHIN *Southampton* which made the inaugural flight of B.O.A.C.'s new Springbok flying-boat service to South Africa in May, 1948.

Registration	Aircraft	Registration	Aircraft	Registration	Aircraft
G-AFMA	D.H. Dragon Rapide of Ciro's Aviation Ltd.	G-AGJV, G-AGJW, G-AGJZ	Douglas Dakota of British European Airways	G-AGSJ	D.H. Dragon Rapide of Island Air Services Ltd.
G-AFMJ	D.H. Dragon Rapide of Air Enterprises Ltd.	G-AGKA, G-AGKB, G-AGKC, G-AGKE, G-AGKF, G-AGKG, G-AGKH, G-AGKI, G-AGKJ, G-AGKK, G-AGKL, G-AGKN	Douglas Dakota of B.O.A.C.	G-AGSK	D.H. Dragon Rapide of British European Airways
G-AFRK	D.H. Dragon Rapide of British European Airways			G-AGSL, G-AGSM, G-AGSN, G-AGSO, G-AGSP	Avro York of B.O.A.C.
G-AFYH	D.H. Flamingo of British Air Transport Ltd.			G-AGUH	Avro Anson of International Airways Ltd.
G-AFZP	Fokker F.22 of Scottish Airlines	G-AGKV, G-AGKW, G-AGKX, G-AGKY, G-AGKZ	Short "Hythe" Flying-boat of B.O.A.C.	G-AGUJ, G-AGUM	Avro Lancaster of British South American Airways
G-AGBG	Lockheed 14 of North Sea Air Transport Ltd.				
G-AGDT	Lockheed 12a of North Sea Air Transport Ltd.	G-AGLA, G-AGLS, G-AGLT	Avro Lancastrian of B.O.A.C.	G-AGUP, G-AGUR, G-AGUU, G-AGUV	D.H. Dragon Rapide of British European Airways
G-AGER, G-AGEU, G-AGEW	Short "Hythe" Flying-boat of B.O.A.C.	G-AGLV	Avro Lancastrian of Skyways Ltd.	G-AGVC	Bristol Freighter of British Aviation Services Ltd.
G-AGGA, G-AGHE, G-AGHF, G-AGHH, G-AGHM, G-AGHN, G-AGHO	Douglas Dakota of B.O.A.C.	G-AGLW, G-AGLY, G-AGMA, G-AGMB, G-AGME, G-AGMG, G-AGMK, G-AGMM	Avro Lancastrian of B.O.A.C.	G-AGWC	D.H. Dragon Rapide of Air Transport (Charter) (C.I.)
G-AGHJ, G-AGHL, G-AGHS	Douglas Dakota of British European Airways			G-AGWI, G-AGWL	Avro Lancastrian of British South American Airways
G-AGHX, G-AGHZ, G-AGIA	Short "Hythe" Flying-boat of B.O.A.C.	G-AGMZ, G-AGNB, G-AGNC, G-AGND, G-AGNE, G-AGNF, G-AGNG, G-AGNK	Douglas Dakota of B.O.A.C.	G-AGWN	Lockheed 12a of Skyways Ltd.
G-AGIF	D.H. Dragon Rapide of Ulster Aviation Ltd.			G-AGWP, G-AGWR	D.H. Dragon Rapide of Morton Air Services Ltd.
G-AGIP, G-AGIS, G-AGIU, G-AGIW, G-AGIX	Douglas Dakota of British European Airways	G-AGNL, G-AGNM, G-AGNN, G-AGNO, G-AGNP, G-AGNS, G-AGNT, G-AGNU		G-AGWS	Douglas Dakota of Scottish Airlines
G-AGIZ	Douglas Dakota of B.O.A.C.			G-AGYX, G-AGYZ, G-AGZB, G-AGZD	Douglas Dakota of British European Airways
G-AGJA, G-AGJB, G-AGJC, G-AGJD, G-AGJE	Avro York of B.O.A.C.	G-AGNV, G-AGNW, G-AGNX, G-AGNY, G-AGNZ, G-AGOA, G-AGOB, G-AGOC, G-AGOD, G-AGOE, G-AGOF	Avro York of B.O.A.C.	G-AGZF, G-AGZG	Douglas Dakota of Scottish Airlines
G-AGJG	D.H. Dragon Rapide of British European Airways			G-AGZJ	D.H. Dragon Rapide of Cambrian Air Services Ltd.
G-AGJJ, G-AGJL, G-AGJM, G-AGJN, G-AGJO	Short "Hythe" Flying-boat of B.O.A.C.	G-AGPH, G-AGSH	D.H. Dragon Rapide of British European Airways	G-AHAG	D.H. Dragon Rapide of North Sea Air Transport Ltd.
G-AGJP	Consolidated Liberator of B.O.A.C.	G-AGSI	D.H. Dragon Rapide of Olley Air Service Ltd.	G-AHBT	Avro Lancastrian of Skyways Ltd.
				G-AHBV	Avro Lancastrian of British Aviation Services Ltd.

29

G-AHBZ G-AHCC	Avro Lancastrian of Skyways Ltd.	G-AHJC	Bristol Wayfarer of British Aviation Services Ltd.	G-AHWF	D.H. Dragon Rapide of Hunting Air Travel Ltd.
G-AHCT G-AHCU G-AHCV G-AHCW G-AHCX G-AHCY G-AHCZ	Douglas Dakota of British European Airways	G-AHJD	Bristol Freighter of Airwork Ltd.	G-AHXK	Avro Anson of Sivewright Airways Ltd.
		G-AHJX	Airspeed Consul of Morton Air Services Ltd.	G-AHXP	Airspeed Consul of International Airways Ltd.
G-AHDY	Consolidated Liberator of Scottish Airlines	G-AHKH	Avro Anson of British Air Transport Ltd.	G-AHXV G-AHXW G-AHXX G-AHXY G-AHXZ	D.H. Dragon Rapide of British European Airways
G-AHDZ	Airspeed Oxford of Scottish Airlines	G-AHKS G-AHKT G-AHKU G-AHKV G-AHLL	D.H. Dragon Rapide of British European Airways	G-AHYB G-AHYD G-AHYE G-AHYF G-AHYG	Consolidated Liberator of B.O.A.C.
G-AHEA	D.H. Dragon Rapide of Lancashire Aircraft Corporation	G-AHLN	D.H. Dragon Rapide of Ulster Aviation Ltd.		
G-AHEH	Airspeed Consul of British Air Transport Ltd.	G-AHLU	D.H. Dragon Rapide of North Sea Air Transport	G-AHYN	Avro Anson of Sivewright Airways Ltd.
G-AHEJ G-AHEK G-AHEL G-AHEM G-AHEN	Lockheed Constellation of B.O.A.C.	G-AHLV	Avro York of Skyways Ltd.	G-AHYY G-AHZA G-AHZC G-AHZD G-AHZE G-AHZF G-AHZG	Short "Plymouth" Flying-boat of B.O.A.C.
G-AHEX G-AHEY G-AHFA G-AHFB G-AHFC G-AHFD G-AHFE G-AHFF G-AHFG G-AHFH	Avro York of British South American Airways	G-AHMB	Airspeed Consul of Dennis Aviation Ltd.		
		G-AHMD	Airspeed Consul of Lancashire Aircraft Corporation	G-AHZH	Consolidated Liberator of Scottish Airlines
		G-AHNJ G-AHNK G-AHNN	Avro Tudor IV of British South American Airways	G-AHZK G-AHZL G-AHZO	Handley Page Halifax of L.A.M.S. Ltd.
G-AHFI	Avro York of Skyways Ltd.			G-AHZP G-AHZR	Consolidated Liberator of Scottish Airlines
G-AHFJ	D.H. Dragon Rapide of Skyways Ltd.	G-AHOY	Vickers Viking of British European Airways		
G-AHFT	Airspeed Consul of Morton Air Services Ltd.	G-AHPI G-AHPJ	Vickers Viking of Hunting Air Travel Ltd.	G-AHZV G-AHZW	Airspeed Consul of Lancashire Aircraft Corporation
G-AHGD	D.H. Dragon Rapide of North Sea Air Transport Ltd.	G-AHPM G-AHPN G-AHPO G-AHPR G-AHPS	Vickers Viking of British European Airways	G-AIAH	Airspeed Consul of Morton Air Services Ltd.
G-AHGG	D.H. Dragon Rapide of Olley Air Service Ltd.	G-AHPT	D.H. Dragon Rapide of Island Air Charters Ltd.	G-AIBF	Airspeed Consul of British Aviation Services Ltd.
G-AHIA	D.H. Dragon Rapide of Morton Air Services Ltd.	G-AHPU	D.H. Dragon Rapide of Hunting Air Travel Ltd.	G-AICV	Douglas Dakota of Skyways Ltd.
G-AHIL G-AHIM G-AHIN G-AHIO G-AHIR G-AHIS G-AHIT G-AHIU G-AHIV G-AHIW G-AHIX G-AHIY	Short Solent Flying-boat of B.O.A.C.	G-AHRB	D.H. Dove of Skyways Ltd.	G-AIDY G-AIDZ G-AIEA	Airspeed Consul of British Air Transport Ltd.
		G-AHRK	Airspeed Consul of British Aviation Services Ltd.	G-AIHV G-AIHX G-AIHY	Handley Page Halifax of Lancs. Aircraft Corporation
		G-AHTY	D.H. Dragon Rapide of North Sea Air Transport Ltd.	G-AIIS	Airspeed Consul of International Airways Ltd.
				G-AIJD	Douglas Dakota of Ciro's Aviation Ltd.

G-AIKO	Airspeed Consul of Chartair Ltd.	G-AIUR	Airspeed Consul of Chartair Ltd.	G-AJAW	Lockheed Lodestar of British Aviation Services Ltd.
G-AIKR	Airspeed Consul of Airwork Ltd.	G-AIUU	Airspeed Consul of International Airways Ltd.	G-AJAY G-AJAZ	Douglas Dakota of Westminster Airways Ltd.
G-AIKT	Airspeed Consul of Ulster Aviation Ltd.	G-AIUV G-AIUW	Airspeed Consul of Hornton Airways Ltd.	G-AJBG G-AJBH	Douglas Dakota of Air Transport (Charter) (C.I.)
G-AIKX	Airspeed Consul of Chartair Ltd.	G-AIUX	Airspeed Consul of Chartair Ltd.	G-AJBI	D.H. Dove of Hunting Air Travel Ltd.
G-AIOB	Avro Anson of WesternAirways				D.H. Dragon Rapide of Birkett Air Services Ltd.
G-AIOL	Airspeed Consul of International Airways Ltd.	G-AIUY	Airspeed Consul of Olley Air Service Ltd.	G-AJBJ	
G-AIOM	Airspeed Consul of Chartair Ltd.	G-AIVB G-AIVC G-AIVD G-AIVF G-AIVG G-AIVH G-AIVI G-AIVJ G-AIVK G-AIVL G-AIVM G-AIVN G-AIVO	Vickers Viking of British European Airways	G-AJBM G-AJBN G-AJBP G-AJBS G-AJBT G-AJBU G-AJBV G-AJBW G-AJBX G-AJBY G-AJCE	Vickers Viking of British European Airways
G-AIOP	Airspeed Consul of Hornton Airways Ltd.				
G-AIOR	Airspeed Consul of Dennis Aviation Ltd.				
G-AIOS	Airspeed Consul of Morton Air Services Ltd.				
G-AIOT	Airspeed Consul of Patrick-Duval AviationServices	G-AIVY	Airspeed Oxford of British South American Airways	G-AJDN	D.H. Dragon Rapide of Birkett Air Services Ltd.
G-AIOU	Airspeed Consul of Morton Air Services Ltd.	G-AIWC G-AIWD G-AIWE	Douglas Dakota of Air Contractors Ltd.	G-AJDP	D.H. Dove of Hunting Air Travel Ltd.
G-AIOV	Airspeed Consul of Patrick-Duval AviationServices	G-AIWF	D.H. Dove of British Aviation Services Ltd.	G-AJFK	D.H. Dragon Rapide of Island Air Charters
G-AIOW	Airspeed Consul of Morton Air Services Ltd.	G-AIWG	D.H. Dragon Rapide of North Sea Air Transport	G-AJFP G-AJFR G-AJFS G-AJFT	Vickers Viking of Airwork Ltd.
G-AIOY	D.H. Dragon Rapide of Island Air Services	G-AIWJ G-AIWK G-AIWP	Handley Page Halifax of L.A.M.S. Ltd.	G-AJFU	D.H. Dragon Rapide of Air Charter Ltd.
G-AIRH	Douglas Dakota of British Aviation Services Ltd.	G-AIWV	Avro Anson of British Air Transport Ltd.	G-AJFX	Avro Anson of Blue Line Airways
G-AIRX	Avro Anson of North Sea Air Transport Ltd.	G-AIWZ	D.H. Dragon Rapide of North Sea Air Transport	G-AJGA	Airspeed Consul of Northern Air Charter Ltd.
G-AISI	Miles Aerovan of British Nederland Air Services Ltd.	G-AIXO	Avro Anson of Culliford Air Lines Ltd.	G-AJGB	Airspeed Consul of International Airways Ltd.
G-AITJ G-AITK	Avro Anson of Western Airways Ltd.	G-AIXR G-AIXS	Vickers Viking of Airwork Ltd.	G-AJGD	Airspeed Consul of Olley Air Service Ltd.
G-AITL	Airspeed Consul of International Airways Ltd.	G-AIXU	Avro Anson of British Air Transport Ltd.	G-AJGG	Airspeed Consul of Chartair Ltd.
G-AIUL	D.H. Dragon Rapide of Air Transport (Charter) (C.I.)	G-AIYE	D.H. Dragon Rapide of Olley Air Service Ltd.	G-AJGH	Airspeed Consul of Air Charter Ltd.
G-AIUO	D.H. Dragon Rapide of Hornton Airways Ltd.	G-AJAV	Douglas Dakota of British Aviation Services Ltd.	G-AJGV	D.H. Dragon Rapide of Manx Air ChartersLtd.
				G-AJHO G-AJHP	D.H. Dragon Rapide of Brooklands Aviation Ltd.

31

G-AJHY, G-AJHZ, G-AJIA, G-AJIB, G-AJIC	Douglas Dakota of British European Airways
G-AJKP	Miles Aerovan of Patrick-Duval Aviation Services
G-AJKU	Miles Aerovan of Ulster Aviation Ltd.
G-AJKW, G-AJKX, G-AJKY	D.H. Dragon Rapide of Lancs. Aircraft Corporation
G-AJLH	Airspeed Consul of Northern Air Charter Ltd.
G-AJLI	Airspeed Consul of Westminster Airways Ltd.
G-AJLJ	Airspeed Consul of Air Enterprises Ltd.
G-AJLK	Airspeed Consul of Birkett Air Services Ltd.
G-AJLR	Airspeed Consul of Olley Air Service Ltd.
G-AJMY	D.H. Dragon Rapide of Sivewright Airways Ltd.
G-AJMZ	Short "Plymouth" Flying-boat of B.O.A.C.
G-AJNG	Airspeed Consul of Westminster Airways Ltd.
G-AJNZ	Handley Page Halifax of World Air Freight Ltd.
G-AJOF	Miles Aerovan of Patrick-Duval Aviation Services
G-AJOI	Miles Aerovan of Sivewright Airways Ltd.
G-AJOT	D.H. Dove of Olley Air Service Ltd.
G-AJPF	Douglas Dakota of Trent Valley Aviation Ltd.
G-AJPL, G-AJPM, G-AJPN, G-AJPO	Douglas Skymaster of Skyways Ltd.
G-AJPP	Avro Lancastrian of Skyways Ltd.
G-AJTU	D.H. Dragon Rapide of Southern Aircraft Ltd.
G-AJVY	Douglas Dakota of Scottish Airlines
G-AJZD	Douglas Dakota of British-Nederland Air Services Ltd.
G-AJZG	Miles Aerovan of Culliford Air Lines Ltd.
G-AJZX	Douglas Dakota of British-Nederland Air Services Ltd.
G-AJZY, G-AJZZ	Handley Page Halifax of Lancs. Aircraft Corporation
G-AKAB	Avro Lancaster of Skyways Ltd.
G-AKAR	Douglas Dakota of Kearsley Airways Ltd.
G-AKAY	Douglas Dakota of Sivewright Airways Ltd.
G-AKCE	Lockheed Constellation of B.O.A.C.
G-AKCO, G-AKCP, G-AKCR	Short Sandringham VII of B.O.A.C.
G-AKDT	Douglas Dakota of Kearsley Airways Ltd.
G-AKEC	Handley Page Halifax of Lancs. Aircraft Corporation
G-AKEW	Avro Anson of Southern Aircraft Ltd.
G-AKFF, G-AKFG	Avro Lancastrian of British South American Airways
G-AKFK, G-AKFL, G-AKFM	Avro Anson of Blue Line Airways
G-AKGH, G-AKGI, G-AKGJ, G-AKGK, G-AKGM	Boeing Stratocruiser of B.O.A.C.
G-AKGV	D.H. Dragon Rapide of Ciro's Aviation Ltd.
G-AKGY	D.H. Dragon Rapide of Manx Air Charters Ltd.
G-AKGZ	Handley Page Halifax of World Air Freight Ltd.
G-AKIF	D.H. Dragon Rapide of Manx Air Charters Ltd.
G-AKIL	Douglas Dakota of Air Transport (Charter) (C.I.) Ltd.
G-AKJG	D.H. Dove of British Aviation Services Ltd.
G-AKJN	Douglas Dakota of Ciro's Aviation Ltd.
G-AKJP	D.H. Dove of British Aviation Services Ltd.
G-AKJR	D.H. Dove of Olley Air Service Ltd.
G-AKLL	Douglas Dakota of Hornton Airways Ltd.
G-AKMW	Avro Lancaster of British South American Airways
G-AKNN	D.H. Dragon Rapide of West Cumberland Air Services
G-AKNV, G-AKNW	D.H. Dragon Rapide of Lancs. Aircraft Corporation
G-AKNX, G-AKNY, G-AKNZ, G-AKOA, G-AKOB	D.H. Dragon Rapide of Air Enterprises Ltd.
G-AKOO	D.H. Dragon Rapide of Southern Aircraft Ltd.
G-AKOY	D.H. Dragon Rapide of Air Navigation & Trading Ltd.
G-AKOZ	Douglas Dakota of Kearsley Airways Ltd.
G-AKPA	D.H. Dragon Rapide of Newman Airways
G-AKPY, G-AKPZ, G-AKRB	Avro Lancastrian of B.O.A.C.
G-AKRG	Supermarine Sea Otter of Air Navigation & Trading Ltd.
G-AKRS	D.H. Dragon Rapide of Air Enterprises Ltd.
G-AKSB, G-AKSD	D.H. Dragon Rapide of Olley Air Service Ltd.

G-AKSE	D.H. Dragon Rapide of Manx AirCharters Ltd.			**LN—NORWAY.**			**NC—U.S.A.**
G-AKSG	D.H. Dragon Rapide of Air Navigation & Trading Ltd.		LN-IAD / LN-IAE	Douglas Skymaster of D.N.L. (S.A.S.)		NC 14747 / NC 34537 / NC 34558 / NC 34577 / NC 44994 / NC 45341 / NC 45342 / NC 45343 / NC 45344 / NC 45345 / NC 45346	Douglas Skymaster of Trans-World Airline
G-AKSK	D.H. Dove of Olley Air Service Ltd.		LN-IAF / LN-IAG / LN-IAH / LN-IAI / LN-IAK / LN-IAL / LN-IAM / LN-IAN	Douglas Dakota of D.N.L. (S.A.S.)			
G-AKSM	Douglas Dakota of Sivewright Airways Ltd.		LN-IAO / LN-IAP / LN-IAR / LN-IAS / LN-IAT			NC 54227 / NC 79008 / NC 79009 / NC 79010	Douglas Dakota of Pan American Airways
G-AKST / G-AKSU	D.H. Dove of Morton Air Services Ltd.		LN-IAU / LN-IAW	Short Sandringham VI of D.N.L. (S.A.S.)		NC 79066 / NC 79067	Douglas Skymaster of Trans-World Airline
G-AKTC / G-AKTG	Avro Lancastrian of British South American Airways		LN-LAG / LN-LAH	Douglas DC-6 of D.N.L. (S.A.S.)		NC 86506 / NC 86511	Lockheed Constellation of Trans-World Airline
G-AKUB / G-AKUC	D.H. Dragon Rapide of Cambrian Air Services		LN-LAI	Short Sandringham VI of D.N.L. (S.A.S.)		NC 86527 / NC 86529 / NC 86530	Lockheed Constellation of Pan American Airways
G-AKUS	D.H. Dragon Rapide of Morton Air Services Ltd.		LN-KAD / LN-KAE / LN-KAF / LN-KAG	Junkers Ju 52/3m of D.N.L. (S.A.S.)		NC 86571	Douglas Skymaster of Trans-World Airline
G-AKYH	Supermarine Sea Otter of Air Navigation & Trading Ltd.			**LV—ARGENTINE.**		NC 88832 / NC 88833 / NC 88836 / NC 88837 / NC 88838 / NC 88846 / NC 88847 / NC 88850 / NC 88855 / NC 88856 / NC 88857 / NC 88859 / NC 88861 / NC 88865 / NC 88868	Lockheed Constellation of Pan American Airways
G-AKZT	D.H. Dragon Rapide of Air Navigation & Trading Ltd.		LV-ABI / LV-ABM / LV-ABN / LV-ABO / LV-ABP / LV-ABQ / LV-ABR / LV-ABS	Douglas Skymaster of F.A.M.A.			
	HB—SWITZERLAND		LV-ACU / LV-ACV	Avro Lancastrian of F.A.M.A.			
HB-ILA / HB-ILE / HB-ILI / HB-ILO	Douglas Skymaster of Swissair		LV-ADH / LV-AEU	Douglas Skymaster of F.A.M.A.		NC 88919 / NC 88927 / NC 88945	Douglas Skymaster of Pan American Airways
HB-IRA / HB-IRB / HB-IRD / HB-IRE / HB-IRF / HB-IRG / HB-IRI / HB-IRK / HB-IRL / HB-IRM / HB-IRN / HB-IRO	Douglas Dakota of Swissair		LV-AEW / LV-AEV	Vickers Viking of F.A.M.A.		NC 90814 / NC 90815 / NC 90816	Lockheed Constellation of Trans-World Airline
			LV-AEU / LV-AFD	Douglas Skymaster of F.A.M.A.			
			LV-AFL / LV-AFF / LV-AFI / LV-AFU	Vickers Viking of F.A.M.A.		NC 90901 / NC 90902 / NC 90903 / NC 90905 / NC 90906 / NC 90909 / NC 90910 / NC 90911 / NC 90912 / NC 90913 / NC 90915	Douglas Skymaster of American Overseas Airlines
HB-IRP / HB-IRR / HB-IRS / HB-IRT	Convair 240 Liner of Swissair		LV-AFV / LV-AFY / LV-AFZ	Avro York of F.A.M.A.			
HB-IRX	Douglas Dakota of Swissair			**LX—LUXEMBOURG**			
HB-ITE / HB-ITO	Douglas DC-2 of Swissair		LX-LAA / LX-LAB	Douglas Dakota of Luxembourg Airlines			

33

NC 90921		OO-AWD	D.H. Dove	PH-TBV	
NC 90922	Lockheed	OO-AWE	of Sabena	PH-TBX	Douglas Dakota
NC 90923	Constellation	OO-CBI		PH-TBY	of K.L.M.
NC 90924	of American	OO-CBJ		PH-TBZ	
NC 90925	Overseas	OO-CBK		PH-TCE	Douglas Sky-
NC 90926	Airlines	OO-CBL	Douglas	PH-TCF	master of K.L.M.
NC 90927		OO-CBM	Skymaster		
NC 91201		OO-CBN	of Sabena	PH-TCI	
NC 91202		OO-CBO		PH-TCK	
NC 91203		OO-CBP		PH-TCL	Douglas Dakota
NC 91204		OO-CBQ		PH-TCS	of K.L.M.
NC 91205	Lockheed	OO-AWF		PH-TCT	
NC 91206	Constellation	OO-AWG	Douglas Dakota	PH-TCU	
NC 91207	of Trans-World	OO-AWK	of Sabena	PH-TDA	
NC 91208	Airline	OO-AWN		PH-TDB	
NC 91209				PH-TDC	
NC 91210				PH-TDD	Lockheed
NC 91211				PH-TDE	Constellation
NC 91212				PH-TDF	of K.L.M.

OK—CZECHO-SLOVAKIA.

		OY-AAB	Douglas Dakota of D.D.L. (S.A.S.)	PH-TDG	
				PH-TDH	
OK-WAA		OY-AAE	Douglas DC-6 of		
OK-WCN		OY-AAF	D.D.L. (S.A.S.)	PH-TDS	
OK-WCO		OY-AOB		PH-TDT	
OK-WCP		OY-AUB		PH-TDU	Douglas Dakota
OK-WCR		OY-AYB		PH-TDV	of K.L.M.
OK-WCS		OY-DCA		PH-TDW	
OK-WCT		OY-DCE		PH-TDZ	
OK-WDA		OY-DCO		PH-TEA	
OK-WDC		OY-DCU	Douglas Dakota	PH-TEB	
OK-WDE		OY-DCY	of D.D.L.	PH-TEC	
OK-WDF		OY-DDA	(S.A.S.)	PH-TED	
OK-WDG		OY-DDE		PH-TEE	
OK-WDH		OY-DDI		PH-TEF	Convair 240
OK-WDI		OY-DDO		PH-TEG	Liner of K.L.M.
OK-WDJ	Douglas Dakota	OY-DDU		PH-TEH	
OK-WDK	of C.S.A.	OY-DDY		PH-TEI	
OK-WDL	(Czech Airlines)	OY-DFI	Douglas	PH-TEK	
OK-WDN		OY-DFO	Skymaster of	PH-TEL	
OK-WDO			D.D.L. (S.A.S.)	PH-TEM	
OK-WDP			Junkers	PH-TEN	
OK-WDQ		OY-DFU	Ju 52/3m of	PH-TEO	Lockheed
OK-WDR			D.D.L. (S.A.S.)	PH-TEP	Constellation
OK-WDS		OY-DLA		PH-TER	of K.L.M.
OK-WDT		OY-DLE	Vickers Viking	PH-TES	
OK-WDU		OY-DLO	of D.D.L. (S.A.S.)	PH-TET	
OK-WDV		OY-DLU		PH-TEU	Douglas Dakota
OK-WDW				PH-TEW	of K.L.M.
OK-WDY		## PH—HOLLAND.		PH-TEY	Douglas Sky-
OK-WDZ				PH-TEZ	master of K.L.M.
OK-XDH		PH-TAH			
OK-XDN		PH-TAM		PH-TPB	
		PH-TAP	Douglas	PH-TPI	
## OO—BELGIUM.		PH-TAR	Skymaster	PH-TPJ	Douglas DC-6
		PH-TAS	of K.L.M.	PH-TPM	of K.L.M.
OO-AUL		PH-TAT		PH-TPP	
OO-AUM		PH-TAU	Lockheed	PH-TPT	
OO-AUN		PH-TAV	Constellation	PH-TLK	
OO-AUO		PH-TAW	of K.L.M.	PH-TLO	Douglas Sky-
OO-AUP		PH-TAY		PH-TLW	master of K.L.M.
OO-AUQ		PH-TAZ		PH-TSC	
OO-AUR	Douglas Dakota	PH-TBG			
OO-AUS	of Sabena	PH-TBH		## PP—BRAZIL.	
OO-AUT		PH-TBI	Douglas Dakota		
OO-AUV		PH-TBK	of K.L.M.		
OO-AUX		PH-TBL		PP-PCB	
OO-AUY		PH-TBM		PP-PCF	Lockheed
OO-AUZ		PH-TBP		PP-PCG	Constellation of
OO-AWA				PP-PCR	Panair do Brasil
OO-AWB	Douglas DC-6	PH-TBU	Douglas Sky-	PP-PDA	
OO-AWC	of Sabena		master of K.L.M.		

SE—SWEDEN.

SE-BAA SE-BAB SE-BAC SE-BAL SE-BAS SE-BAT SE-BAU SE-BAW SE-BAZ	Douglas Dakota of A.B.A. (S.A.S.)
SE-BBA SE-BBC SE-BBD SE-BBE SE-BBF SE-BBG	Douglas Skymaster of A.B.A. (S.A.S.)
SE-BBH SE-BBI SE-BBK SE-BBL SE-BBM SE-BBN SE-BBO SE-BBP SE-BBR	Douglas Dakota of A.B.A. (S.A.S.)

SE-BDB SE-BDC SE-BDD SE-BDE SE-BDF SE-BDL SE-BDM SE-BDO	Douglas DC-6 of A.B.A. (S.A.S.)

SX—GREECE.

SX-BBA SX-BBB SX-BBC SX-BBD	Douglas Dakota of Hellenic Airlines
SX-DAA	Consolidated Liberator of Hellenic Airlines

VH—AUSTRALIA.

VH-EAA VH-EAB VH-EAC VH-EAD	Lockheed Constellation of Qantas Empire Airways

VP—SOUTHERN RHODESIA.

VP-YEW VP-YEX YP-YEY VP-YHJ VP-YHT	Vickers Viking of Central African Airways

VT—INDIA.

VT-CQS VT-CQT VT-CQU	Lockheed Constellation of Air India International

YI—IRAQ.

YI-ABP YI-ABQ YI-ABR	Vickers Viking of Iraqi Airways

ZS—SOUTH AFRICA

ZS-AUA ZS-AUG ZS-BMF ZS-BMG ZS-BMH ZS-BWN	Douglas Skymaster of South African Airways

DYCE AIRPORT (ABERDEEN).

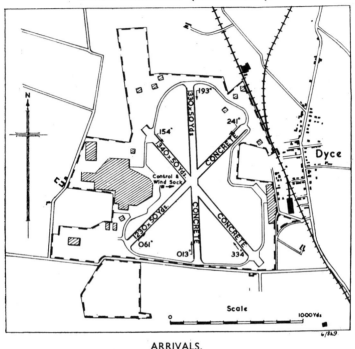

ARRIVALS.

Time	Frequency	Aircraft	From
10.55 a.m.	Weekdays	B.E.A. Rapide	Orkney
11.35 a.m.	Weekdays	B.E.A. Rapide	Shetland
12.20 p.m.	Weekdays	B.E.A. Dakota	London (Northolt)
2.45 p.m.	Weekdays	B.E.A. Rapide	Wick
3.20 p.m.	Weekdays	B.E.A. Rapide	Orkney
5.15 p.m.	Weekdays	B.E.A. Rapide	Wick
5.40 p.m.	Weekdays	B.E.A. Dakota	Orkney
6.40 p.m.	Weekdays	B.E.A. Rapide	Orkney

DEPARTURES.

Time	Frequency	Aircraft	To
8.00 a.m.	Weekdays	B.E.A. Rapide	Orkney
8.50 a.m.	Weekdays	B.E.A. Rapide	Shetland
12.30 p.m.	Weekdays	B.E.A. Dakota	Orkney
12.30 p.m.	Weekdays	B.E.A. Rapide	Wick
1.15 p.m.	Weekdays	B.E.A. Rapide	Orkney
3.00 p.m.	Weekdays	B.E.A. Rapide	Shetland
3.05 p.m.	Weekdays	B.E.A. Rapide	Wick
3.45 p.m.	Weekdays	B.E.A. Rapide	Orkney
6.00 p.m.	Weekdays	B.E.A. Dakota	London (Northolt)

NUTT'S CORNER AIRPORT (BELFAST).

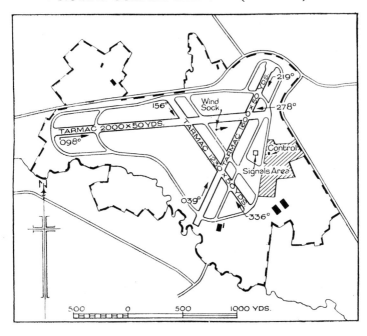

ARRIVALS.

Time	Frequency	Aircraft	From
9.30 a.m.	Weekdays	B.E.A. Dakota	Renfrew (Glasgow)
9.50 a.m.	Weekdays	B.E.A. Dakota	Liverpool
11.40 a.m.	Weekdays	B.E.A. Dakota	Northolt (London)
12.15 noon	Daily	B.E.A. Dakota	Manchester
12.55 noon	Daily	B.E.A. Dakota	Renfrew (Glasgow)
1.25 p.m.	Weekdays	B.E.A. Dakota	Liverpool
4.40 p.m.	Daily	B.E.A. Dakota	Renfrew (Glasgow)
5.40 p.m.	Daily	B.E.A. Dakota	Liverpool
6.16 p.m.	Weekdays	B.E.A. Dakota	Northolt (London)
7.15 p.m.	Weekdays	B.E.A. Dakota	Manchester
7.40 p.m.	Weekdays	B.E.A. Dakota	Renfrew (Glasgow)
8.04 p.m.	Sunday	B.E.A. Dakota	Northolt (London)
9.40 p.m.	Weekdays	B.E.A. Dakota	Northolt (London)

DEPARTURES.

Time	Frequency	Aircraft	To
8.49 a.m.	Weekdays	B.E.A. Dakota	Northolt (London)
10.15 a.m.	Weekdays	B.E.A. Dakota	Liverpool
10.25 a.m.	Weekdays	B.E.A. Dakota	Renfrew (Glasgow)
12.50 noon	Daily	B.E.A. Dakota	Manchester
1.01 p.m.	Weekdays	B.E.A. Dakota	Northolt (London)
2.15 p.m.	Daily	B.E.A. Dakota	Renfrew (Glasgow)

Time	Frequency	Aircraft	To
2.30 p.m.	Daily	B.E.A. Dakota	Liverpool
2.35 p.m.	Sunday	B.E.A. Dakota	Northolt (London)
5.15 p.m.	Daily	B.E.A. Dakota	Renfrew (Glasgow)
6.10 p.m.	Daily	B.E.A. Dakota	Liverpool
7.01 p.m.	Weekdays	B.E.A. Dakota	Northolt (London)
7.45 p.m.	Weekdays	B.E.A. Dakota	Manchester
8.15 p.m.	Weekdays	B.E.A. Dakota	Renfrew (Glasgow)

SQUIRE'S GATE AIRPORT (BLACKPOOL).

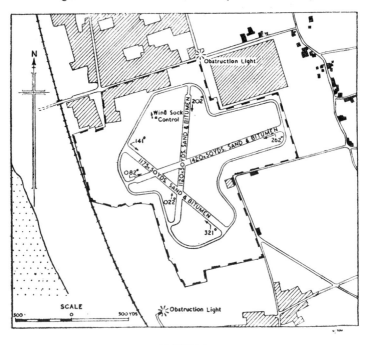

ARRIVALS.

Time	Frequency	Aircraft	From
2.05 p.m.	Daily	B.E.A. Dakota	Isle of Man
6.40 p.m.	Daily	B.E.A. Dakota	Isle of Man

DEPARTURES.

Time	Frequency	Aircraft	To
2.30 p.m.	Daily	B.E.A. Dakota	Isle of Man
7.05 p.m.	Daily	B.E.A. Dakota	Isle of Man

PENGAM MOORS AIRPORT (CARDIFF).

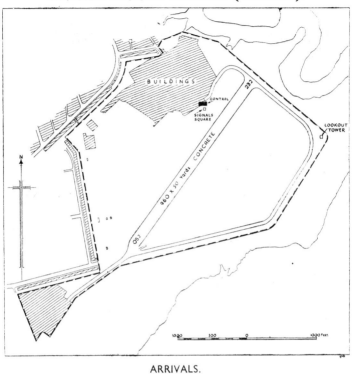

ARRIVALS.

Time	Frequency	Aircraft	From
9.00 a.m.	Daily	Western Airways Anson	Weston
9.45 a.m.	Daily	Cambrian Air Services Rapide	Weston
12.30 noon	Daily	Western Airways Anson	Weston
4.45 p.m.	Daily	Cambrian Air Services Rapide	Weston
6.45 p.m.	Daily	Western Airways Anson	Weston
9.15 p.m.	Daily	Cambrian Air Services Rapide	Weston

DEPARTURES.

Time	Frequency	Aircraft	To
9.00 a.m.	Daily	Cambrian Air Services Rapide	Weston
11.00 a.m.	Daily	Western Airways Anson	Weston
12.45 noon	Daily	Cambrian Air Services Rapide	Weston
3.00 p.m.	Daily	Western Airways Anson	Weston
6.00 p.m.	Daily	Cambrian Air Services Rapide	Weston
9.00 p.m.	Daily	Western Airways Anson	Weston

CROYDON AIRPORT.

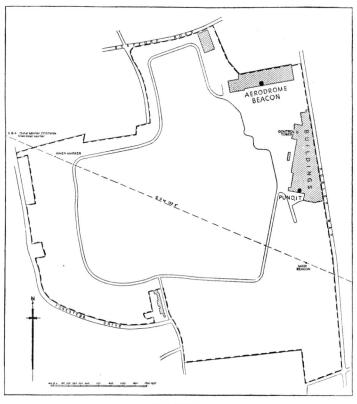

ARRIVALS.

Time	Frequency	Aircraft	From
10.45 a.m.	Weekdays	Air Transport Beechcraft	Deauville
11.05 a.m.	Weekdays	Air Transport Beechcraft	Lille
12.30 noon	Weekdays	Olley Air Service Rapide	Deauville
4.20 p.m.	Daily	Air Transport Beechcraft	Deauville
7.45 p.m.	Daily	Olley Air Service Rapide	Deauville

DEPARTURES.

Time	Frequency	Aircraft	To
10.00 a.m.	Sunday	Olley Air Service Rapide	Deauville
10.00 a.m.	Weekdays	Olley Air Service Rapide	Deauville
11.35 a.m.	Weekdays	Air Transport Beechcraft	Deauville
4.00 p.m.	Weekdays	Olley Air Service Rapide	Deauville
4.40 p.m.	Weekdays	Air Transport Beechcraft	Lille
6.45 p.m.	Daily	Air Transport Beechcraft	Deauville

COLLINSTOWN AIRPORT (DUBLIN).

ARRIVALS.

Time	Frequency	Aircraft	From
9.00 a.m.	Daily	Aer Lingus Dakota	Northolt (London)
10.00 a.m.	Daily	Aer Lingus Dakota	Northolt (London)
10.15 a.m.	Daily	Aer Lingus Dakota	Liverpool
10.25 a.m.	Daily	Aer Lingus Dakota	Renfrew (Glasgow)
10.50 a.m.	Daily	Aer Lingus Dakota	Amsterdam
11.30 a.m.	Daily	Aer Lingus Dakota	Northolt (London)
12.30 noon	Daily	Aer Lingus Dakota	Northolt (London)
1.00 p.m.	Daily	Aer Lingus Dakota	Isle of Man
2.00 p.m.	Daily	Aer Lingus Dakota	Northolt (London)
2.35 p.m.	Daily	Aer Lingus Dakota	Amsterdam
2.55 p.m.	Daily	Aer Lingus Dakota	Renfrew (Glasgow)
3.00 p.m.	Daily	Aer Lingus Dakota	Northolt (London)
4.15 p.m.	Daily	Aer Lingus Dakota	Liverpool
4.20 p.m.	Mon., Wed., Sun.	Aer Lingus Dakota	Paris
4.40 p.m.	Daily	Aer Lingus Dakota	Northolt (London)
5.30 p.m.	Daily	Aer Lingus Dakota	Northolt (London)
6.25 p.m.	Daily	Aer Lingus Dakota	Renfrew (Glasgow)
6.45 p.m.	Daily	Aer Lingus Dakota	Shannon
7.10 p.m.	Daily	Aer Lingus Dakota	Northolt (London)
7.30 p.m.	Daily	Aer Lingus Dakota	Liverpool
7.40 p.m.	Mon., Tues., Sun.	K.L.M. Dakota	Amsterdam
7.40 p.m.	Thur., Fri., Sat.	Aer Lingus Dakota	Amsterdam
8.20 p.m.	Daily	Aer Lingus Dakota	Northolt (London)
8.30 p.m.	Tues, Thurs.	S.A.B.E.N.A. Dakota	Brussels
9.40 p.m.	Daily	Aer Lingus Dakota	Northolt (London)
10.15 p.m.	Sat., Sun.	Aer Lingus Dakota	Isle of Man
10.45 p.m.	Daily	Aer Lingus Dakota	Liverpool
10.50 p.m.	Daily	Aer Lingus Dakota	Northolt (London)

DEPARTURES.

Time	Frequency	Aircraft	To
7.00 a.m.	Daily	Aer Lingus Dakota	Northolt (London)
7.15 a.m.	Mon., Fri., Sat.	Aer Lingus Dakota	Renfrew (Glasgow)
7.30 a.m.	Daily	Aer Lingus Dakota	Liverpool
7.45 a.m.	Daily	Aer Lingus Dakota	Amsterdam
8.00 a.m.	Daily	Aer Lingus Dakota	Northolt (London)
8.15 a.m.	Mon., Wed., Sun.	Aer Lingus Dakota	Paris
8.30 a.m.	Wed., Fri.	S.A.B.E.N.A. Dakota	Brussels
8.40 a.m.	Thurs., Fri., Sat.	Aer Lingus Dakota	Amsterdam
8.40 a.m.	Mon., Tues., Wed.	K.L.M. Dakota	Amsterdam
8.45 a.m.	Daily	Aer Lingus Dakota	Shannon
9.30 a.m.	Daily	Aer Lingus Dakota	Northolt (London)
10.30 a.m.	Daily	Aer Lingus Dakota	Northolt (London)
11.30 a.m.	Daily	Aer Lingus Dakota	Manchester
11.45 a.m.	Daily	Aer Lingus Dakota	Renfrew (Glasgow)
12.10 noon	Daily	Aer Lingus Dakota	Northolt (London)
1.00 p.m.	Daily	Aer Lingus Dakota	Northolt (London)
1.30 p.m.	Daily	Aer Lingus Dakota	Liverpool
2.30 p.m.	Daily	Aer Lingus Dakota	Northolt (London)
3.15 p.m.	Daily	Aer Lingus Dakota	Renfrew (Glasgow)
3.45 p.m.	Daily	Aer Lingus Dakota	Northolt (London)
4.45 p.m.	Daily	Aer Lingus Dakota	Liverpool
5.10 p.m.	Daily	Aer Lingus Dakota	Northolt (London)
6.20 p.m.	Daily	Aer Lingus Dakota	Northolt (London)
7.00 p.m.	Daily	Aer Lingus Dakota	Manchester
7.40 p.m.	Daily	Aer Lingus Dakota	Northolt (London)
8.00 p.m.	Daily	Aer Lingus Dakota	Liverpool
8.15 p.m.	Sat., Sun.	Aer Lingus Dakota	Isle of Man
8.50 p.m.	Daily	Aer Lingus Dakota	Northolt (London)

TURNHOUSE AIRPORT (EDINBURGH).

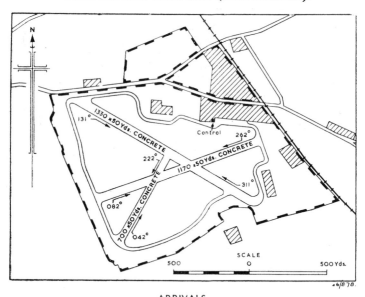

ARRIVALS.

Time	Frequency	Aircraft	From
9.05 a.m.	Weekdays	B.E.A. Dakota	Renfrew (Glasgow)
11.08 a.m.	Weekdays	B.E.A. Dakota	Northolt (London)
6.50 p.m.	Weekdays	B.E.A. Dakota	Orkney
9.23 p.m.	Weekdays	B.E.A. Dakota	Northolt (London)

DEPARTURES.

Time	Frequency	Aircraft	To
9.26 a.m.	Weekdays	B.E.A. Dakota	Northolt (London)
11.30 a.m.	Weekdays	B.E.A. Dakota	Orkney
7.10 p.m.	Weekdays	B.E.A. Dakota	Northolt (London)
9.50 p.m.	Weekdays	B.E.A. Dakota	Renfrew (Glasgow)

GATWICK AIRPORT.

ARRIVALS.

Time	Frequency	Aircraft	From
3.15 p.m.	Saturdays	Air Transport Beechcraft or Bristol 170	Dinard

DEPARTURES.

Time	Frequency	Aircraft	To
12.00 noon	Saturdays	Air Transport Beechcraft or Bristol 170	Dinard

SPEKE AIRPORT (LIVERPOOL).

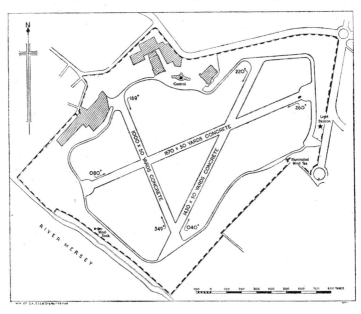

ARRIVALS.

Time	Frequency	Aircraft	From
8.45 a.m.	Weekdays	B.E.A. Dakota	Isle of Man
9.05 a.m.	Daily	Aer Lingus Dakota	Dublin
10.35 a.m.	Daily	B.E.A. Dakota	Isle of Man
11.30 a.m.	Weekdays	B.E.A. Dakota	Belfast
12.35 p.m.	Daily	Aer Lingus Dakota	Dublin
3.00 p.m.	Daily	B.E.A. Dakota	Isle of Man
3.45 p.m.	Daily	B.E.A. Dakota	Belfast
4.05 p.m.	Daily	Aer Lingus Dakota	Dublin
4.45 p.m.	Daily	B.E.A. Dakota	Isle of Man
7.10 p.m.	Mon., Fri., Sat., Sun.	B.E.A. Dakota	Isle of Man
7.50 p.m.	Daily	Aer Lingus Dakota	Dublin
8.00 p.m.	Daily	B.E.A. Dakota	Belfast
8.50 p.m.	Daily	Aer Lingus Dakota	Dublin
9.30 p.m.	Daily	B.E.A. Dakota	Isle of Man

DEPARTURES.

Time	Frequency	Aircraft	To
8.00 a.m.	Weekdays	B.E.A. Dakota	Belfast
9.15 a.m.	Daily	B.E.A. Dakota	Isle of Man
9.45 a.m.	Daily	Aer Lingus Dakota	Dublin
11.50 a.m.	Daily	B.E.A. Dakota	Isle of Man
1.15 p.m.	Daily	Aer Lingus Dakota	Dublin
3.30 p.m.	Daily	B.E.A. Dakota	Isle of Man
4.15 p.m.	Daily	B.E.A. Dakota	Belfast
4.50 p.m.	Daily	Aer Lingus Dakota	Dublin
5.05 p.m.	Daily	B.E.A. Dakota	Isle of Man

Time	Frequency	Aircraft	To
7.35 p.m.	Mon., Fri., Sat., Sun.	B.E.A. Dakota	Isle of Man
8.30 p.m.	Daily	Aer Lingus Dakota	Dublin
9.20 p.m.	Daily	Aer Lingus Dakota	Dublin
9.30 p.m.	Daily	B.E.A. Dakota	Isle of Man

LONDON AIRPORT (HEATHROW).

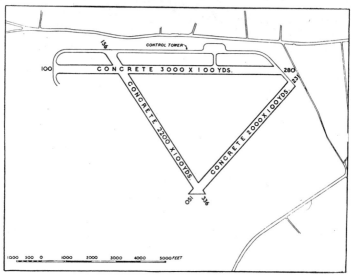

ARRIVALS.

MONDAY

Time	Aircraft	From
00.35 a.m.	Panair Constellation	Buenos Aires
7.45 a.m.	B.O.A.C. York	Calcutta
8.50 a.m.	K.L.M. Skymaster	Amsterdam
8.50 a.m.	Sabena Dakota	Brussels
9.55 a.m.	Air France Languedoc 161	Paris
10.35 a.m.	B.O.A.C. York	Accra (West Africa)
11.10 a.m.	Sabena Dakota	Antwerp
11.20 a.m.	K.L.M. Skymaster	Amsterdam
11.55 a.m.	Air France Languedoc 161	Paris
12.00 noon	Sabena Dakota	Brussels
1.10 p.m.	Sabena Dakota	Brussels
1.20 p.m.	K.L.M. Skymaster	Amsterdam
2.20 p.m.	P.A.A. Constellation	New York
2.35 p.m.	T.C.A. North Star	Montreal
2.55 p.m.	Air France Languedoc 161	Paris
2.55 p.m.	Sabena Dakota	Brussels
3.20 p.m.	K.L.M. Skymaster	Amsterdam
3.35 p.m.	B.S.A.A.C. York	Buenos Aires
4.30 p.m.	A.O.A. Skymaster	Frankfurt
4.55 p.m.	Air France Languedoc 161	Paris

Avro Tudor IV G-AHNK *Star Lion* at London Airport. British South American Airways has three Tudor IV airliners in service and other Tudors of a later type on order.

Star Glitter, G-AHFH, one of the ten Avro York Mk. IG airliners on the British South American Airways route to Buenos Aires, via Lisbon, Dakar and Rio de Janeiro.

Avro Lancastrian II *Star Flight* of British South American Airways. Lancastrians now serve mainly for freight duties.

(Photos: A. S. C. Lumsden

Upper: Regular visitor to ̄Prestwick and Ringway, the C.O.B.E.T.A. Dakota OO-APC from Brussels.
Lower: C.S.A. (Czech Airlines) Dakota from Prague at Northolt Airport.

(Photos: A. S. C. Lumsden

Upper: Douglas Dakota G-AKIK of Cyprus Airways, a new airline company operating as a subsidiary of B.E.A.C. Three Dakotas are in service.
Lower: Avro York LV-AFV of the Argentine airline F.A.M.A. which flies into London Airport on the trunk route from Buenos Aires, calling at Rio, Natal, Dakar, Madrid, Rome and Paris.

Upper: One of F.A.M.A.'s five Douglas DC-4B Skymasters which operate to this country over the same route as the company's three Yorks.

(Photo: A. S. C. Lumsden

Lower: Maid of Athens, a Consolidated Liberator flown into Northolt and Prestwick from Athens by Hellenic Airlines.   *(Photo: Scottish Avn.*

(Photos: A. S. C. Lumsden

Upper: The Spanish airline "Iberia" now operates the London-Madrid service with Douglas Skymasters.   Illustrated is EC-ACE, one of three aircraft of this type in service.

Lower: K.L.M. Skymaster PH-TLK at London Airport.

Flying Dutchman PH-TDW, one of the twenty-seven Douglas DC-3 Dakota airliners in service with K.L.M. This machine operates the Eindhoven-London schedules.

Luxembourg Airlines Douglas Dakota at Northolt on arrival from Luxembourg. This company is partially owned by Scottish Aviation Ltd.

(*Photos: A. S. C. Lumsden*

This Pan American World Airways Constellation is a familiar sight at London Airport. *Clipper Challenge* NC 88837 is on the regular Atlantic crossing from New York.

Time	Aircraft	From
5.00 p.m.	Sabena Dakota	Knocke/Le Zoute
5.00 p.m.	B.O.A.C. Dakota	Cairo
5.20 p.m.	C.S.A. Dakota	Prague
5.20 p.m.	K.L.M. Skymaster	Amsterdam
6.35 p.m.	P.A.A. Dakota	Vienna
7.10 p.m.	Sabena Dakota	Brussels
7.20 p.m.	K.L.M. Skymaster	Amsterdam
7.55 p.m.	Air France Languedoc 161	Paris
8.55 p.m.	Air France Languedoc 161	Paris
9.40 p.m.	K.L.M. Dakota	Eindhoven
9.50 p.m.	Air France Languedoc 161	Nice
10.05 p.m.	P.A.A. Constellation	New York
10.20 p.m.	K.L.M. Skymaster	Amsterdam
10.30 p.m.	Sabena Dakota	Prague
10.40 p.m.	Sabena Dakota	Brussels

TUESDAY

Time	Aircraft	From
8.50 a.m.	K.L.M. Skymaster	Amsterdam
8.50 a.m.	Sabena Dakota	Brussels
9.55 a.m.	Air France Languedoc 161	Paris
10.35 a.m.	B.O.A.C. York	Accra (West Africa)
11.10 a.m.	Sabena Dakota	Brussels
11.20 a.m.	K.L.M. Skymaster	Amsterdam
12.00 noon	Sabena Dakota	Brussels
1.10 p.m.	Sabena Dakota	Brussels
1.20 p.m.	K.L.M. Skymaster	Amsterdam
1.25 p.m.	A.O.A. Constellation	New York
2.20 p.m.	P.A.A. Constellation	New York
2.35 p.m.	T.C.A. North Star	Montreal
2.45 p.m.	B.O.A.C. Liberator	Montreal
2.55 p.m.	Air France Languedoc 161	Paris
2.55 p.m.	Sabena Dakota	Brussels
3.15 p.m.	B.O.A.C. Constellation	New York
3.20 p.m.	K.L.M. Skymaster	Amsterdam
4.55 p.m.	Air France Languedoc 161	Paris
5.00 p.m.	B.O.A.C. Dakota	Cairo
5.00 p.m.	Sabena Dakota	Knocke/Le Zoute
5.30 p.m.	K.L.M. Skymaster	Amsterdam
6.30 p.m.	B.O.A.C. Constellation	Montreal
6.35 p.m.	P.A.A. Dakota	Vienna
7.00 p.m.	B.S.A.A.C. Lancastrian	Santiago (Chile)
7.10 p.m.	Sabena Dakota	Brussels
7.10 p.m.	C.S.A. Dakota	Prague
7.20 p.m.	K.L.M. Skymaster	Amsterdam
7.25 p.m.	B.O.A.C. York	Tanganyika
7.55 p.m.	P.A.A. Constellation	Istanbul
7.55 p.m.	Languedoc 161 Air France	Paris
8.15 p.m.	B.O.A.C. Lancastrian Freighter	Johannesburg
8.55 p.m.	Air France Languedoc 161	Paris
9.40 p.m.	K.L.M. Dakota	Eindhoven
10.20 p.m.	K.L.M. Dakota	Prague
10.20 p.m.	K.L.M. Skymaster	Amsterdam
10.40 p.m.	Sabena Dakota	Brussels

WEDNESDAY

Time	Aircraft	From
7.45 a.m.	B.O.A.C. York	Calcutta
8.50 a.m.	K.L.M. Skymaster	Amsterdam
8.50 a.m.	Sabena Dakota	Brussels
9.55 a.m.	Air France Languedoc 161	Paris
10.20 a.m.	South African Skymaster	Johannesburg
11.10 a.m.	Sabena Dakota	Brussels
11.20 a.m.	K.L.M. Skymaster	Amsterdam
11.55 a.m.	Air France Languedoc 161	Paris
12.00 noon	Sabena Dakota	Brussels
1.10 p.m.	Sabena Dakota	Brussels
1.20 p.m.	K.L.M. Skymaster	Amsterdam
1.25 p.m.	A.O.A. Constellation	New York

Time	Aircraft	From
2.05 p.m.	P.A.A. Constellation	New York
2.20 p.m.	P.A.A. Constellation	New York
2.35 p.m.	T.C.A. North Star	Montreal
2.55 p.m.	Air France Languedoc 161	Paris
2.55 p.m.	Sabena Dakota	Brussels
3.20 p.m.	K.L.M. Skymaster	Amsterdam
4.30 p.m.	A.O.A. Skymaster	Frankfurt
4.55 p.m.	Air France Languedoc 161	Paris
5.00 p.m.	B.O.A.C. Dakota	Cairo
5.00 p.m.	Sabena Dakota	Brussels
5.20 p.m.	C.S.A. Dakota	Prague
5.20 p.m.	K.L.M. Skymaster	Amsterdam
6.16 p.m.	Qantas Constellation	Sydney (Australia)
6.30 p.m.	P.A.A. Skymaster Freighter	Brussels
6.35 p.m.	P.A.A. Dakota	Vienna
7.10 p.m.	Sabena Dakota	Brussels
7.20 p.m.	K.L.M. Skymaster	Amsterdam
7.25 p.m.	B.O.A.C. York	Nairobi
7.30 p.m.	Air India Constellation	Bombay
7.55 p.m.	P.A.A. Constellation	Calcutta
7.55 p.m.	Air France Languedoc 161	Paris
8.55 p.m.	Air France Languedoc 161	Paris
9.40 p.m.	K.L.M. Dakota	Eindhoven
9.50 p.m.	Air France Languedoc 161	Nice
10.05 p.m.	P.A.A. Constellation	New York
10.20 p.m.	K.L.M. Skymaster	Amsterdam
10.40 p.m.	Sabena Dakota	Brussels

THURSDAY

Time	Aircraft	From
5.30 a.m.	K.L.M. Skymaster	Amsterdam
6.55 a.m.	A.O.A. Constellation	New York
8.50 a.m.	K.L.M. Skymaster	Amsterdam
8.50 a.m.	Sabena Dakota	Brussels
9.55 a.m.	Air France Languedoc 161	Paris
10.05 a.m.	P.A.A. Constellation	New York
10.35 a.m.	B.O.A.C. York	Accra (West Africa)
11.10 a.m.	Sabena Dakota	Brussels
11.20 a.m.	K.L.M. Skymaster	Amsterdam
12.00 noon	Sabena Dakota	Brussels
1.10 p.m.	Sabena Dakota	Brussels
1.20 p.m.	K.L.M. Skymaster	Amsterdam
1.25 p.m.	A.O.A. Constellation	New York
2.20 p.m.	P.A.A. Constellation	New York
2.35 p.m.	T.C.A. North Star	Montreal
2.45 p.m.	B.O.A.C. Liberator	Montreal
2.55 p.m.	Air France Languedoc 161	Paris
2.55 p.m.	Sabena Dakota	Brussels
3.20 p.m.	P.A.A. Dakota	Vienna
3.20 p.m.	K.L.M. Skymaster	Amsterdam
3.35 p.m.	B.S.A.A.C. York	Buenos Aires
4.55 p.m.	Air France Languedoc 161	Paris
5.00 p.m.	B.O.A.C. Dakota	Cairo
5.00 p.m.	Sabena Dakota	Brussels
5.20 p.m.	K.L.M. Skymaster	Amsterdam
6.30 p.m.	B.O.A.C. Constellation	Montreal
7.10 p.m.	Sabena Dakota	Brussels
7.10 p.m.	C.S.A. Dakota	Prague
7.20 p.m.	K.L.M. Skymaster	Amsterdam
7.55 p.m.	Air France Languedoc 161	Paris
8.55 p.m.	Air France Languedoc 161	Paris
9.40 p.m.	K.L.M. Dakota	Eindhoven
10.20 p.m.	K.L.M. Dakota	Prague
10.20 p.m.	K.L.M. Skymaster	Amsterdam
10.40 p.m.	Sabena Dakota	Brussels

FRIDAY

Time	Aircraft	From
7.45 a.m.	B.O.A.C. York	Calcutta

Time	Aircraft	From
8.50 a.m.	K.L.M. Skymaster	Amsterdam
8.50 a.m.	Sabena Dakota	Brussels
9.55 a.m.	Air France Languedoc 161	Paris
10.05 a.m.	P.A.A. Constellation	New York
10.20 a.m.	South African Skymaster	Johannesburg
10.25 a.m.	A.O.A. Skymaster	New York
10.35 a.m.	B.O.A.C. York	Accra (West Africa)
11.10 a.m.	Sabena Dakota	Antwerp
11.20 a.m.	K.L.M. Skymaster	Amsterdam
11.55 a.m.	Air France Languedoc 161	Paris
12.00 noon	Sabena Dakota	Brussels
1.10 p.m.	Sabena Dakota	Brussels
1.20 p.m.	K.L.M. Skymaster	Amsterdam
1.25 p.m.	A.O.A. Constellation	New York
2.20 p.m.	P.A.A. Constellation	New York
2.35 p.m.	T.C.A. North Star	Montreal
2.45 p.m.	B.O.A.C. Liberator	Montreal
2.55 p.m.	Air France Languedoc 161	Paris
2.55 p.m.	Sabena Dakota	Brussels
3.15 p.m.	B.O.A.C. Constellation	New York
3.20 p.m.	K.L.M. Skymaster	Amsterdam
4.30 p.m.	A.O.A. Skymaster	Frankfurt
4.55 p.m.	Air France Languedoc 161	Paris
5.00 p.m.	B.O.A.C. Dakota	Cairo
5.00 p.m.	Sabena Dakota	Knocke/Le Zoute
5.20 p.m.	C.S.A. Dakota	Prague
5.20 p.m.	K.L.M. Skymaster	Amsterdam
6.35 p.m.	P.A.A. Dakota	Vienna
7.10 p.m.	Sabena Dakota	Brussels
7.20 p.m.	K.L.M. Skymaster	Amsterdam
7.25 p.m.	B.O.A.C. York	Nairobi
7.55 p.m.	P.A.A. Constellation	Calcutta
7.55 p.m.	Air France Languedoc 161	Paris
8.55 p.m.	Air France Languedoc 161	Paris
9.40 p.m.	K.L.M. Dakota	Eindhoven
9.50 p.m.	Air France Languedoc 161	Nice
10.05 p.m.	P.A.A. Constellation	New York
10.20 p.m.	K.L.M. Skymaster	Amsterdam
10.30 p.m.	Sabena Dakota	Prague
10.40 p.m.	Sabena Dakota	Brussels

SATURDAY.

Time	Aircraft	From
5.30 a.m.	K.L.M. Skymaster	Amsterdam
7.30 a.m.	B.O.A.C. Lancastrian Freighter	Sydney (Australia)
7.30 a.m.	B.O.A.C.	Colombo
7.45 a.m.	B.O.A.C. York	Delhi
8.50 a.m.	K.L.M. Skymaster	Amsterdam
8.50 a.m.	Sabena Dakota	Brussels
9.55 a.m.	Air France Languedoc 161	Paris
10.35 a.m.	B.O.A.C. York	Accra (West Africa)
11.10 a.m.	Sabena Dakota	Antwerp
11.20 a.m.	K.L.M. Skymaster	Amsterdam
11.55 a.m.	Air France Languedoc 161	Paris
12.00 noon	Sabena Dakota	Brussels
1.10 p.m.	Sabena Dakota	Brussels
1.20 p.m.	K.L.M. Skymaster	Amsterdam
1.25 p.m.	A.O.A. Constellation	Washington
1.40 p.m.	Iberia Skymaster	Madrid
2.05 p.m.	P.A.A. Constellation	New York
2.35 p.m.	T.C.A. North Star	Montreal
2.45 p.m.	B.O.A.C. Constellation	New York
2.55 p.m.	Air France Languedoc 161	Paris
2.55 p.m.	Sabena Dakota	Brussels
3.20 p.m.	P.A.A. Dakota	Vienna
3.20 p.m.	K.L.M. Skymaster	Amsterdam
3.35 p.m.	B.S.A.A.C. York	Buenos Aires
4.35 p.m.	B.O.A.C. Dakota	Teheran
4.55 p.m.	Air France Languedoc 161	Paris

Time	Aircraft	From
5.00 p.m.	Sabena Dakota	Knocke/Le Zoute
5.00 p.m.	B.O.A.C. Dakota	Cairo
5.20 p.m.	K.L.M. Skymaster	Amsterdam
5.50 p.m.	P.A.A. Constellation	New York
6.30 p.m.	B.O.A.C. Constellation	Montreal
7.10 p.m.	Sabena Dakota	Brussels
7.10 p.m.	C.S.A. Dakota	Prague
7.20 p.m.	K.L.M. Skymaster	Amsterdam
7.25 p.m.	B.O.A.C. York	Nairobi
7.55 p.m.	Air France Languedoc 161	Paris
8.55 p.m.	Air France Languedoc 161	Paris
9.00 p.m.	B.S.A.A.C. Lancastrian	Havana (Cuba)
9.40 p.m.	K.L.M. Dakota	Eindhoven
9.50 p.m.	Air France Languedoc 161	Nice
10.05 p.m.	P.A.A. Constellation	New York
10.20 p.m.	K.L.M. Dakota	Prague
10.20 p.m.	K.L.M. Skymaster	Amsterdam
10.40 p.m.	Sabena Dakota	Brussels

SUNDAY.

Time	Aircraft	From
7.00 a.m.	Skyways Skymaster	Bahrein
7.30 a.m.	B.O.A.C. York	Colombo
8.40 a.m.	A.O.A. Constellation	New York
8.50 a.m.	K.L.M. Skymaster	Amsterdam
9.55 a.m.	Air France Languedoc 161	Paris
10.20 a.m.	South African Skymaster	Johannesburg
11.20 a.m.	K.L.M. Skymaster	Amsterdam
12.00 noon	Sabena Dakota	Brussels
1.10 p.m.	Sabena Dakota	Brussels
1.20 p.m.	K.L.M. Skymaster	Amsterdam
1.25 p.m.	A.O.A. Constellation	New York
2.20 p.m.	P.A.A. Constellation	New York
2.35 p.m.	T.C.A. North Star	Montreal
2.45 p.m.	F.A.M.A. York or Skymaster	Buenos Aires
2.55 p.m.	Air France Languedoc 161	Paris
2.55 p.m.	Sabena Dakota	Brussels
3.20 p.m.	P.A.A. Dakota	Vienna
3.20 p.m.	K.L.M. Skymaster	Amsterdam
3.35 p.m.	B.S.A.A.C. York	Rio de Janeiro
4.55 p.m.	Air France Languedoc 161	Paris
5.00 p.m.	Sabena Dakota	Knocke/Le Zoute
5.20 p.m.	K.L.M. Skymaster	Amsterdam
5.30 p.m.	B.O.A.C. Dakota	Cairo
7.00 p.m.	B.S.A.A.C. Lancastrian	Nassau (West Indies)
7.10 p.m.	Sabena Dakota	Brussels
7.20 p.m.	K.L.M. Skymaster	Amsterdam
7.25 p.m.	B.O.A.C. York	Tanganyika
7.55 p.m.	Air France Languedoc 161	Paris
8.55 p.m.	Air France Languedoc 161	Paris
10.05 p.m.	P.A.A. Constellation	New York
10.20 p.m.	K.L.M. Dakota	Prague
10.20 p.m.	K.L.M. Skymaster	Amsterdam
10.30 p.m.	P.A.A. Skymaster Freighter	New York
10.30 p.m.	Sabena Dakota	Prague
10.40 p.m.	Sabena Dakota	Brussels

DEPARTURES.

MONDAY

Time	Aircraft	To
7.45 a.m.	Sabena Dakota	Brussels
8.00 a.m.	K.L.M. Dakota	Eindoven
8.15 a.m.	B.O.A.C. York	Nairobi
8.30 a.m.	K.L.M. Skymaster	Amsterdam
9.05 a.m.	Air France Languedoc 161	Paris
10.00 a.m.	B.O.A.C. Dakota	Cairo
10.00 a.m.	Sabena Dakota	Brussels

LONDON AIRPORT—*contd.*

Time	Aircraft	To
10.25 a.m.	B.S.A.A.C. York	Buenos Aires
10.30 a.m.	P.A.A. Dakota	Vienna
10.30 a.m.	K.L.M. Skymaster	Amsterdam
11.00 a.m.	Panair do Brasil Constellation	Buenos Aires
11.05 a.m.	Air France Languedoc 161	Paris
12.00 noon	South African Skymaster	Johannesburg
12.00 noon	Sabena Dakota	Brussels
12.30 noon	C.S.A. Dakota	Prague
12.30 noon	K.L.M. Skymaster	Amsterdam
12.50 noon	Sabena Dakota	Knocke/Le Zoute
12.55 noon	Air France Languedoc 161	Nice
1.01 p.m.	P.A.A. Constellation	New York
1.45 p.m.	B.O.A.C. York	Accra (West Africa)
2.30 p.m.	Sabena Dakota	Antwerp
2.30 p.m.	K.L.M. Skymaster	Amsterdam
3.45 p.m.	Sabena Dakota	Brussels
4.05 p.m.	Air France Languedoc 161	Paris
4.30 p.m.	K.L.M. Skymaster	Amsterdam
5.55 p.m.	Sabena Dakota	Brussels
6.05 p.m.	Air France Languedoc 161	Paris
6.30 p.m.	A.O.A. Constellation	New York
6.30 p.m.	K.L.M. Skymaster	Amsterdam
7.00 p.m.	B.O.A.C. Constellation	New York
7.45 p.m.	Sabena Dakota	Prague
8.30 p.m.	K.L.M. Skymaster	Amsterdam
8.45 p.m.	P.A.A. Constellation	New York
9.05 p.m.	Air France Languedoc 161	Paris
10.00 p.m.	T.C.A. North Star	Montreal
10.00 p.m.	Sabena Dakota	Antwerp

TUESDAY

Time	Aircraft	To
1.10 a.m.	K.L.M. Skymaster	Amsterdam
7.45 a.m.	Sabena Dakota	Brussels
8.00 a.m.	K.L.M. Dakota	Eindhoven
8.15 a.m.	B.O.A.C. York	Nairobi
8.30 a.m.	B.O.A.C. York	Tanganyika
8.30 a.m.	K.L.M. Skymaster	Amsterdam
8.30 a.m.	K.L.M. Dakota	Prague
9.05 a.m.	Air France Languedoc 161	Paris
10.00 a.m.	B.O.A.C. Dakota	Cairo
10.00 a.m.	Sabena Dakota	Brussels
10.20 a.m.	Air France Languedoc 161	Paris
10.30 a.m.	P.A.A. Dakota	Vienna
10.30 a.m.	K.L.M. Skymaster	Amsterdam
11.05 a.m.	Air France Languedoc 161	Paris
12.00 noon	Sabena Dakota	Brussels
12.30 noon	K.L.M. Skymaster	Amsterdam
12.50 noon	Sabena Dakota	Knocke/Le Zoute
12.55 noon	B.S.A.A.C. Lancastrian	Havana (Cuba)
1.01 p.m.	P.A.A. Constellation	New York
1.45 p.m.	B.O.A.C. York	Accra (West Africa)
2.30 p.m.	Sabena Dakota	Antwerp
2.30 p.m.	K.L.M. Skymaster	Amsterdam
2.30 p.m.	C.S.A. Dakota	Prague
2.45 p.m.	B.O.A.C. York	Delhi
3.45 p.m.	Sabena Dakota	Brussels
4.05 p.m.	Air France Languedoc 161	Paris
4.30 p.m.	K.L.M. Skymaster	Amsterdam
5.30 p.m.	A.O.A. Skymaster	Frankfurt
5.55 p.m.	Sabena Dakota	Brussels
6.05 p.m.	Air France Languedoc 161	Paris
6.30 p.m.	A.O.A. Constellation	New York
6.30 p.m.	K.L.M. Skymaster	Amsterdam
7.00 p.m.	B.O.A.C. Constellation	New York
8.30 p.m.	K.L.M. Skymaster	Amsterdam
8.45 p.m.	P.A.A. Constellation	New York
9.05 p.m.	Air France Languedoc 161	Paris
10.00 p.m.	Sabena Dakota	Brussels

53

Time	Aircraft	To
10.00 p.m.	P.A.A. Constellation	New York
10.00 p.m.	B.O.A.C. Constellation	Montreal
10.00 p.m.	T.C.A. North Star	Montreal

WEDNESDAY

1.10 a.m.	K.L.M. Skymaster	Amsterdam
7.45 a.m.	Sabena Dakota	Brussels
8.00 a.m.	K.L.M. Dakota	Eindhoven
8.30 a.m.	K.L.M. Skymaster	Amsterdam
9.05 a.m.	Air France Languedoc 161	Paris
10.00 a.m.	B.O.A.C. Dakota	Cairo
10.00 a.m.	Sabena Dakota	Brussels
10.25 a.m.	B.S.A.A.C. York	Buenos Aires
10.30 a.m.	P.A.A. Dakota	Vienna
10.30 a.m.	K.L.M. Skymaster	Amsterdam
11.05 a.m.	Air France Languedoc 161	Paris
12.00 noon	Sabena Dakota	Brussels
12.30 noon	C.S.A. Dakota	Prague
12.30 noon	K.L.M. Skymaster	Amsterdam
12.50 noon	Sabena Dakota	Knocke/Le Zoute
12.55 noon	Air France Languedoc 161	Nice
1.00 p.m.	Qantas Constellation	Sydney (Australia)
1.01 p.m.	P.A.A. Constellation	New York
1.45 p.m.	B.O.A.C. York	Accra (West Africa)
2.05 p.m.	P.A.A. Constellation	Calcutta
2.30 p.m.	Sabena Dakota	Antwerp
2.30 p.m.	K.L.M. Skymaster	Amsterdam
2.45 p.m.	B.O.A.C. York	Calcutta
3.45 p.m.	Sabena Dakota	Brussels
4.05 p.m.	Air France Languedoc 161	Paris
4.30 p.m.	K.L.M. Skymaster	Amsterdam
5.00 p.m.	B.O A.C. Liberator	Montreal
5.55 p.m.	Sabena Dakota	Brussels
6.05 p.m.	Air France Languedoc 161	Paris
6.30 p.m.	A.C.A. Constellation	New York
6.30 p.m.	K.L.M. Skymaster	Amsterdam
7.00 p.m.	B.O.A.C. Constellation	New York
7.45 p.m.	P.A.A. Skymaster Freighter	New York
7.55 p.m.	A.O.A. Constellation	Frankfurt
8.30 p.m.	K.L.M. Skymaster	Amsterdam
8.45 p.m.	P.A.A. Constellation	New York
9.05 p.m.	Air France Languedoc 161	Paris
10.00 p.m.	Sabena Dakota	Brussels
10.00 p.m.	T.C.A. North Star	Montreal
10.00 p.m.	P.A.A. Constellation	New York

THURSDAY

1.10 a.m.	K.L.M. Skymaster	Amsterdam
7.45 a.m.	Sabena Dakota	Brussels
8.00 a.m.	K.L.M. Dakota	Eindhoven
8.30 a.m.	B.O.A.C. York	Tanganyika
8.30 a.m.	K.L.M. Dakota	Prague
8.30 a.m.	K.L.M. Dakota	Amsterdam
9.05 a.m.	Air France Languedoc 161	Paris
10.00 a.m.	Sabena Dakota	Brussels
10.00 a.m.	B.O.A.C. Dakota	Cairo
10.20 a.m.	Air France Languedoc 161	Paris
10.25 a.m.	B.S.A.A.C. Lancastrian	Nassau (West Indies)
10.30 a.m.	P.A.A. Dakota	Vienna
10.30 a.m.	K.L.M. Skymaster	Amsterdam
11.05 a.m.	Air France Languedoc 161	Paris
12.00 noon	South African Skymaster	Johannesburg
12.00 noon	Sabena Dakota	Brussels
12.30 noon	K.L.M. Skymaster	Amsterdam
12.50 noon	Sabena Dakota	Knocke/Le Zoute
1.01 p.m.	P.A.A. Constellation	New York
2.30 p.m.	Sabena Dakota	Antwerp

54

Time	*Aircraft*	*To*
2.30 p.m.	K.L.M. Skymaster	Amsterdam
2.30 p.m.	C.S.A. Dakota	Prague
3.45 p.m.	Sabena Dakota	Brussels
4.05 p.m.	Air France Languedoc 161	Paris
4.30 p.m.	K.L.M. Skymaster	Amsterdam
5.30 p.m.	A.O.A. Skymaster	Frankfurt
5.55 p.m.	Sabena Dakota	Brussels
6.05 p.m.	Air France Languedoc 161	Paris
6.30 p.m.	A.O.A. Constellation	New York
6.30 p.m.	K.L.M. Skymaster	Amsterdam
8.30 p.m.	K.L.M. Skymaster	Amsterdam
8.45 p.m.	P.A.A. Constellation	New York
9.05 p.m.	Air France Languedoc 161	Paris
10.00 p.m.	Sabena Dakota	Brussels
10.00 p.m.	B.O.A.C. Constellation	Montreal
10.00 p.m.	T.C.A. North Star	Montreal

FRIDAY

7.45 a.m.	Sabena Dakota	Brussels
8.00 a.m.	K.L.M. Dakota	Eindhoven
8.30 a.m.	K.L.M. Skymaster	Amsterdam
9.05 a.m.	Air France Languedoc 161	Paris
10.00 a.m.	B.O.A.C. Dakota	Cairo
10.00 a.m.	Sabena Dakota	Brussels
10.25 a.m.	B.S.A.A.C. York	Buenos Aires
10.30 a.m.	P.A.A. Dakota	Vienna
10.30 a.m.	K.L.M. Skymaster	Amsterdam
10.45 a.m.	B.O.A.C. Dakota	Cairo
11.05 a.m.	Air France Languedoc 161	Paris
12.00 noon	Sabena Dakota	Brussels
12.30 noon	K.L.M. Skymaster	Amsterdam
12.30 noon	C.S.A. Dakota	Prague
12.50 noon	Sabena Dakota	Knocke/Le Zoute
12.55 noon	Air France Languedoc 161	Nice
1.00 p.m.	Qantas Constellation	Sydney (Australia)
1.01 p.m.	P.A.A. Constellation	New York
1.45 p.m.	B.O.A.C. York	Accra
2.30 p.m.	K.L.M. Skymaster	Amsterdam
2.30 p.m.	Sabena Dakota	Antwerp
2.45 p.m.	B.O.A.C. York	Calcutta
3.45 p.m.	Sabena Dakota	Brussels
4.00 p.m.	Air India Constellation	Bombay
4.05 p.m.	Air France Languedoc 161	Paris
4.30 p.m.	K.L.M. Skymaster	Amsterdam
5.30 p.m.	Skyways Skymaster	Behrein
5.55 p.m.	Sabena, Dakota	Brussels
6.05 p.m.	Air France Languedoc 161	Paris
6.30 p.m.	K.L.M. Skymaster	Amsterdam
6.30 p.m.	A.O.A. Constellation	New York
7.00 p.m.	B.O.A.C. Constellation	New York
7.45 p.m.	Sabena Dakota	Prague
8.30 p.m.	K.L.M. Skymaster	Amsterdam
8.45 p.m.	P.A.A. Constellation	New York
9.05 p.m.	Air France Languedoc 161	Paris
10.00 p.m.	Sabena Dakota	Brussels
10.00 p.m.	A.O.A. Skymaster	New York
10.00 p.m.	T.C.A. North Star	Montreal

SATURDAY

7.45 a.m.	Sabena Dakota	Brussels
8.00 a.m.	K.L.M. Dakota	Eindhoven
8.15 a.m.	B.O.A.C. York	Nairobi
8.30 a.m.	K.L.M. Dakota	Prague
8.30 a.m.	K.L.M. Skymaster	Amsterdam
9.05 a.m.	Air France Languedoc 161	Paris
9.40 a.m.	A.O.A. Constellation	Frankfurt
10.00 a.m.	B.O.A.C. Dakota	Cairo
10.00 a.m.	Sabena Dakota	Brussels

Time	Aircraft	To
10.25 a.m.	B.S.A.A.C. Lancastrian	Santiago (Chile
10.30 a.m.	P.A.A. Dakota	Vienna
10.30 a.m.	K.L.M. Skymaster	Amsterdam
11.00 a.m.	F.A.M.A. Skymaster or York	Buenos Aires
11.05 a.m.	Air France Languedoc 161	Paris
12.00 noon	Sabena Dakota	Brussels
12.00 noon	South African Skymaster	Johannesburg
12.30 noon	K.L.M. Skymaster	Amsterdam
12.50 noon	Sabena Dakota	Knocke/Le Zoute
12.55 noon	Air France Languedoc 161	Nice
1.01 p.m.	P.A.A. Constellation	New York
1.45 p.m.	B.O.A.C. York	Accra (West Africa)
2.05 p.m.	P.A.A. Constellation	Calcutta
2.30 p.m.	Sabena Dakota	Antwerp
2.30 p.m.	K.L.M. Skymaster	Amsterdam
2.30 p.m.	C.S.A. Dakota	Prague
3.15 p.m.	Iberia Skymaster	Madrid
3.45 p.m.	Sabena Dakota	Brussels
4.05 p.m.	Air France Languedoc 161	Paris
5.00 p.m.	B.O.A.C. Liberator	Montreal
5.15 p.m.	B.O.A.C. York	Colombo
5.55 p.m.	Sabena Dakota	Brussels
6.05 p.m.	Air France Languedoc 161	Paris
6.30 p.m.	K.L.M. Skymaster	Amsterdam
6.30 p.m.	A.O.A. Constellation	New York
7.00 p.m.	B.O.A.C. Constellation	New York
8.30 p.m.	K.L.M. Skymaster	Amsterdam
8.45 p.m.	P.A.A. Constellation	New York
9.05 p.m.	Air France Languedoc 161	Paris
10.00 p.m.	Sabena Dakota	Brussels
10.00 p.m.	B.O.A.C. Constellation	Montreal
10.00 p.m.	T.C.A. North Star	Montreal

SUNDAY

Time	Aircraft	To
7.45 a.m.	Sabena Dakota	Brussels
8.30 a.m.	K.L.M. Skymaster	Amsterdam
8.30 a.m.	K.L.M. Dakota	Prague
9.05 a.m.	Air France Languedoc 161	Paris
9.20 a.m.	B.O.A.C. Dakota	Teheran
10.00 a.m.	B.O.A.C. Dakota	Cairo
10.20 a.m.	Air France Languedoc 161	Paris
10.30 a.m.	K.L.M. Skymaster	Amsterdam
10.30 a.m.	P.A.A. Skymaster Freighter	Brussels
11.05 a.m.	Air France Languedoc 161	Paris
12.30 noon	K.L.M. Skymaster	Amsterdam
12.50 noon	Sabena Dakota	Knocke/Le Zoute
1.01 p.m.	P.A.A. Constellation	New York
2.00 p.m.	Sabena Dakota	Brussels
2.30 p.m.	K.L.M. Skymaster	Amsterdam
2.45 p.m.	B.O.A.C. York	Calcutta
3.45 p.m.	Sabena Dakota	Brussels
4.05 p.m.	Air France Languedoc 161	Paris
4.30 p.m.	K.L.M. Skymaster	Amsterdam
5.00 p.m.	B.O.A.C. Lancastrian Freighter	Johannesburg
5.30 p.m.	A.O.A. Skymaster	Frankfurt
5.55 p.m.	Sabena Dakota	Brussels
6.05 p.m.	Air France Languedoc 161	Paris
6.30 p.m.	K.L.M. Skymaster	Amsterdam
6.30 p.m.	A.O.A. Constellation	New York
7.00 p.m.	B.O.A.C. Constellation	New York
7.45 p.m.	B.O.A.C. Lancastrian Freighter	Sydney (Australia)
7.45 p.m.	Sabena Dakota	Prague
8.30 p.m.	K.L.M. Skymaster	Amsterdam
8.45 p.m.	P.A.A. Constellation	New York
9.05 p.m.	Air France Languedoc 161	Paris
10.00 p.m.	Sabena Dakota	Brussels
10.00 p.m.	P.A.A. Constellation	New York
10.00 p.m.	T.C.A. North Star	Montreal

RINGWAY AIRPORT (MANCHESTER).

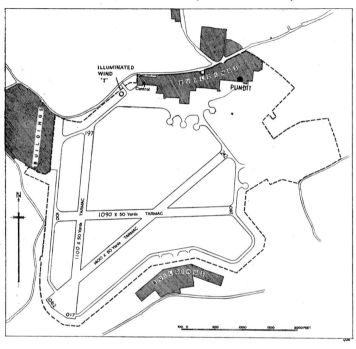

ARRIVALS.

Time	Frequency	Aircraft	From
9.00 a.m.	Daily	Aer Lingus Dakota	Dublin
9.10 a.m.	Tues., Sat.	C.O.B.E.T.A. Dakota	Prestwick (Glasgow)
9.55 a.m.	Mon., Tues., Wed.	K.L.M. Dakota	Dublin
9.55 a.m.	Thur., Fri., Sat.	Aer Lingus Dakota	Dublin
10.25 a.m.	Daily	B.E.A. Dakota	Isle of Man
12.45 p.m.	Daily	Aer Lingus Dakota	Dublin
2.15 p.m.	Daily	B.E.A. Dakota	Belfast
5.10 p.m.	Daily	B.E.A. Dakota	Isle of Man
5.30 p.m.	Mon., Fri.	C.O.B.E.T.A. Dakota	Brussels
5.45 p.m.	Mon., Tues., Sun.	K.L.M. Dakota	Amsterdam
5.45 p.m.	Thur., Fri., Sat.	Aer Lingus Dakota	Amsterdam
8.15 p.m.	Daily	Aer Lingus Dakota	Dublin
9.10 p.m.	Weekdays	B.E.A. Dakota	Belfast
9.35 p.m.	Mon., Tues., Wed., Thur., Fri., Sun.	Air France Languedoc 161	Paris

DEPARTURES.

Time	Frequency	Aircraft	To
8.10 a.m.	Weekdays	B.E.A. Dakota	Isle of Man
9.15 a.m.	Weekdays	Air France Languedoc 161	Paris
9.30 a.m.	Daily	Aer Lingus Dakota	Dublin

RINGWAY AIRPORT—*contd.*

Time	Frequency	Aircraft	To
10.00 a.m.	Tues., Sat.	C.O.B.E.T.A. Dakota	,Brussels
10.30 a.m.	Mon., Tues., Wed.	K.L.M. Dakota	Amsterdam
10.30 a.m.	Thurs., Fri., Sat.	Aer Lingus Dakota	Amsterdam
10.45 a.m.	Daily	B.E.A. Dakota	Belfast
1.15 p.m.	Daily	Aer Lingus Dakota	Dublin
2.35 p.m.	Weekdays	B.E.A. Dakota	Isle of Man
5.45 p.m.	Weekdays	B.E.A. Dakota	Belfast
6.15 p.m.	Mon., Tues., Sun.	K.L.M. Dakota	Dublin
6.15 p.m.	Thurs., Fri., Sat.	Aer Lingus Dakota	Dublin
8.45 p.m.	Daily	Aer Lingus Dakota	Dublin

NORTHOLT AIRPORT

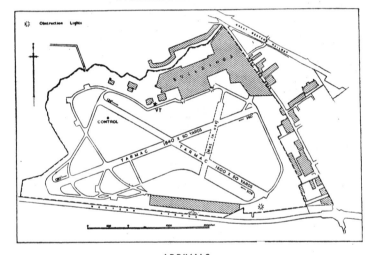

ARRIVALS.

Time	Frequency	Aircraft	From
5.30 a.m.	Wed., Sat.	Hellenic Liberator	Glasgow
8.30 a.m.	Daily	B.E.A. Viking	Amsterdam
9.00 a.m.	Daily	Aer Lingus Dakota	Dublin
9.22 a.m.	Daily	B.E.A. Dakota	Jersey
9.28 a.m.	Daily	B.E.A. Dakota	Guernsey
10.00 a.m.	Daily	Aer Lingus Dakota	Dublin
10.22 a.m.	Daily	B.E.A. Viking	Paris
10.58 a.m.	Weekdays	B.E.A. Viking	Glasgow
11.04 a.m.	Weekdays	B.E.A. Dakota	Belfast
11.16 a.m.	Tues., Sat., Sun.	S.A.S. Viking	Copenhagen
11.22 a.m.	Daily	B.E.A. Dakota	Jersey
11.30 a.m.	Daily	Aer Lingus Dakota	Dublin
11.40 a.m.	Sunday	Swissair Skymaster	Geneva
11.46 a.m.	Weekdays	B.E.A. Viking	Glasgow
11.52 a.m.	Sunday	B.E.A. Viking	Glasgow
11.58 a.m.	Sunday	B.E.A. Dakota	Jersey
12.04 noon	Daily	B.E.A. Viking	Brussels
12.16 noon	Daily	Swissair Skymaster	Zurich
12.22 noon	Mon., Fri., Sat., Sun.	B.E.A. Dakota	Jersey
12.28 noon	Daily	B.E.A. Viking	Paris

Time	Frequency	Aircraft	From
12.30 noon	Daily	Aer Lingus Dakota	Dublin
12.40 noon	Daily	B.E.A. Viking	Copenhagen
12.55 noon	Daily	Aer Lingus Dakota	Shannon
1.04 p.m.	Mon., Wed., Fri.	Swissair Dakota Freighter	Basle
1.22 p.m.	Daily	B.E.A. Dakota	Jersey
1.34 p.m.	Daily	S.A.S. Dakota	Oslo
1.52 p.m.	Tues., Thurs., Sat.	Swissair Dakota	Berne
1.58 p.m.	Weekdays	B.E.A. Viking	Glasgow
2.10 p.m.	Daily	Aer Lingus Dakota	Dublin
2.34 p.m.	Daily	S.A.S. DC-6	Stockholm
2.46 p.m.	Daily	B.E.A. Viking	Stockholm
3.00 p.m.	Daily	Aer Lingus Dakota	Dublin
3.04 p.m.	Tues., Sat.	Alitalia S.M. 95	Rome
3.10 p.m.	Daily	B.E.A. Viking	Paris
3.16 p.m.	Daily	B.E.A. Dakota	Belfast
3.22 p.m.	Daily	B.E.A. Dakota	Jersey
3.28 p.m.	Wednesday	Alitalia S.M. 95	Rome
3.46 p.m.	Mon., Wed., Fri., Sun.	S.A.S. Dakota	Gothenburg
3.52 p.m.	Weekdays	Swissair Dakota	Geneva
4.04 p.m.	Weekdays	B.E.A. Viking	Zurich
4.16 p.m.	Daily	B.E.A. Dakota	Guernsey
4.22 p.m.	Mon., Fri., Sat., Sun.	B.E.A. Dakota	Jersey
4.30 p.m.	Daily	Aer Lingus Dakota	Dublin
4.40 p.m.	Sunday	B.E.A. Dakota	Belfast
4.52 p.m.	Mon., Fri., Sat., Sun.	B.E.A. Dakota	Jersey
5.04 p.m.	Daily	B.E.A. Viking	Paris
5.16 p.m.	Daily	Swissair Dakota	Zurich
5.22 p.m.	Mon., Tues., Thurs., Sat.	C.S.A. Dakota	Prague
5.28 p.m.	Daily	B.E.A. Viking	Brussels
5.30 p.m.	Thurs., Sun.	Hellenic Liberator	Athens
5.34 p.m.	Daily	B.E.A. Dakota	Jersey
5.45 p.m.	Daily	Aer Lingus Dakota	Dublin
6.10 p.m.	Tues., Fri.	B.E.A. Viking	Gibraltar
6.40 p.m.	Weekdays	B.E.A. Dakota	Isle of Ma
6.46 p.m.	Mon., Wed., Fri.	B.E.A. Viking	Oslo
6.52 p.m.	Tues., Wed., Thur., Fri., Sat., Sun.	B.E.A. Viking	Berlin
6.58 p.m.	Mon., Wed., Fri.	B.E.A. Viking	Prague
7.10 p.m.	Daily	Aer Lingus Dakota	Dublin
7.16 p.m.	Wed., Sun.	B.E.A. Viking	Malta and Rome
7.28 p.m.	Wed., Sat.	Luxembourg Dakota	Luxembourg
7.40 p.m.	Tues., Thur., Sat.	B.E.A. Viking	Nice
7.52 p.m.	Tues., Thur., Sat.	Swissair Dakota	Zurich
7.58 p.m.	Daily	B.E.A. Dakota	Jersey
8.04 p.m.	Weekdays	B.E.A. Viking	Vienna
8.10 p.m.	Daily	B.E.A. Viking	Paris
8.16 p.m.	Daily	B.E.A. Dakota	Jersey
8.20 p.m.	Daily	Aer Lingus Dakota	Dublin
8.28 p.m.	Weekdays	B.E.A. Viking	Glasgow
8.34 p.m.	Daily	B.E.A. Viking	Geneva
8.46 p.m.	Sunday	B.E.A. Dakota	Guernsey
8.52 p.m.	Mon., Fri., Sat., Sun.	B.E.A. Dakota	Jersey
8.58 p.m.	Mon., Wed., Sat.	B.E.A. Viking	Madrid
9.04 p.m.	Mon., Wed., Fri.	S.A.S. Dakota	Oslo
9.10 p.m.	Daily	B.E.A. Viking	Brussels
9.16 p.m.	Weekdays	B.E.A. Dakota	Belfast
9.28 p.m.	Wed., Sat.	B.E.A. Viking	Istanbul
9.34 p.m.	Weekdays	B.E.A. Dakota	Orkney
9.40 p.m.	Daily	Aer Lingus Dakota	Dublin
10.10 p.m.	Daily	B.E.A. Viking	Paris
10.16 p.m.	Mon., Wed., Thur., Fri., Sun.	B.E.A. Viking	Athens
10.22 p.m.	Mon., Tues., Thurs., Sat., Sun.	B.E.A. Viking	Lisbon
10.50 p.m.	Daily	Aer Lingus Dakota	Dublin

DEPARTURES.

Time	Frequency	Aircraft	To
5.30 a.m.	Daily	B.E.A. Dakota	Guernsey
5.30 a.m.	Daily	B.E.A. Dakota	Jersey
7.00 a.m.	Daily	Aer Lingus Dakota	Dublin
7.00 a.m.	Wed., Sat.	Hellenic Liberator	Athens
7.57 a.m.	Mon., Wed., Sat.	B.E.A. Viking	Madrid
8.00 a.m.	Daily	Aer Lingus Dakota	Dublin
8.00 a.m.	Daily	B.E.A. Dakota	Jersey
8.09 p.m.	Daily	B.E.A. Viking	Brussels
8.12 a.m.	Tues., Sat.	B.E.A. Viking	Rome and Malta
8.15 a.m.	Daily	B.E.A. Viking	Paris
8.21 a.m.	Mon., Tues., Thurs., Fri., Sat.	B.E.A. Viking	Lisbon
8.24 a.m.	Tues., Thur., Fri., Sun.	C.S.A. Dakota	Prague
8.30 a.m.	Daily	B.E.A. Viking	Amsterdam
8.33 a.m.	Sunday	B.E.A. Dakota	Jersey
8.39 a.m.	Tues., Wed., Thurs., Fri., Sat., Sun.	B.E.A. Viking	Berlin
8.45 a.m.	Daily	B.E.A. Viking	Zurich
8.48 a.m.	Weekdays	B.E.A. Dakota	Orkney
8.54 a.m.	Wed., Fri., Sun.	Swissair Dakota	Zurich
9.00 a.m.	Mon., Fri., Sat., Sun.	B.E.A. Dakota	Jersey
9.03 a.m.	Weekdays	B.E.A. Viking	Glasgow
9.15 a.m.	Daily	B.E.A. Dakota	Belfast
9.21 a.m.	Mon., Wed., Fri.	B.E.A. Viking	Oslo
9.30 a.m.	Daily	Aer Lingus Dakota	Dublin
9.30 a.m.	Thurs., Sun.	Luxembourg Dakota	Luxembourg
9.39 a.m.	Mon., Wed., Fri.	B.E.A. Viking	Prague
9.54 a.m.	Tues., Thurs., Sat.	B.E.A. Viking	Nice
9.57 a.m.	Wed. Thurs., Sun.	Alitalia S.M. 95	Rome
10.00 a.m.	Daily	B.E.A. Dakota	Jersey
10.06 a.m.	Daily	B.E.A. Dakota	Guernsey
10.27 a.m.	Tues., Thurs., Sat.	S.A.S. Dakota	Oslo
10.30 a.m.	Daily	Aer Lingus Dakota	Dublin
11.15 a.m.	Daily	B.E.A. Viking	Paris
11.51 a.m.	Daily	B.E.A. Dakota	Isle of Man
12.00 noon	Daily	Aer Lingus Dakota	Dublin
12.00 noon	Daily	B.E.A. Dakota	Jersey
12.33 noon	Tues., Sat., Sun.	S.A.S. Viking	Copenhagen
12.51 noon	Sunday	Swissair Skymaster	Geneva
1.00 p.m.	Daily	Aer Lingus Dakota	Dublin
1.00 p.m.	Mon., Fri., Sat., Sun.	B.E.A. Dakota	Jersey
1.06 p.m.	Daily	B.E.A. Viking	Brussels
1.15 p.m.	Daily	B.E.A. Viking	Paris
1.21 p.m.	Daily	Swissair Skymaster	Zurich
1.27 p.m.	Daily	B.E.A. Viking	Geneva
1.30 p.m.	Mon., Fri., Sat., Sun.	B.E.A. Dakota	Jersey
1.33 p.m.	Daily	B.E.A. Viking	Copenhagen
1.39 p.m.	Daily	B.E.A. Viking	Stockholm
2.10 p.m.	Daily	Aer Lingus Dakota	Shannon
2.12 p.m.	Mon., Wed., Fri., Sun.	Swissair Dakota Freighter	Zurich
2.15 p.m.	Daily	B.E.A. Dakota	Jersey
2.30 p.m.	Daily	S.A.S. Dakota	Oslo
2.39 p.m.	Mon., Wed., Fri.	Swissair Dakota	Berne
2.39 p.m.	Thurs., Sat., Sun.	Swissair Dakota	Basle
2.40 p.m.	Daily	Aer Lingus Dakota	Dublin
3.03 p.m.	Weekdays	B.E.A. Viking	Glasgow
3.09 p.m.	Daily	S.A.S. Viking or Skymaster	Copenhagen
3.30 p.m.	Daily	Aer Lingus Dakota	Dublin
3.51 p.m.	Daily	B.E.A. Dakota	Belfast
4.00 p.m.	Daily	B.E.A. Dakota	Guernsey
4.15 p.m.	Daily	B.E.A. Viking	Paris
4.21 p.m.	Daily	S.A.S. DC-6	Stockholm
4.33 p.m.	Mon., Wed., Fri., Sun.	S.A.S. Dakota	Gothenburg

Time	Frequency	Aircraft	To
4.39 p.m.	Weekdays	Swissair Dakota	Geneva
4.45 p.m.	Daily	B.E.A. Dakota	Jersey
5.03 p.m.	Sunday	B.E.A. Dakota	Guernsey
5.10 p.m.	Daily	Aer Lingus Dakota	Dublin
5.15 p.m.	Daily	B.E.A. Viking	Brussels
5.30 p.m.	Mon., Fri., Sat., Sun.	B.E.A. Dakota	Jersey
5.39 p.m.	Sunday	B.E.A. Dakota	Belfast
6.05 p.m.	Daily	B.E.A. Dakota	Jersey
6.15 p.m.	Daily	B.E.A. Viking	Paris
6.20 p.m.	Daily	Aer Lingus Dakota	Dublin
7.03 p.m.	Weekdays	B.E.A. Dakota	Glasgow (via Edinburgh)
7.09 p.m.	Daily	B.E.A. Viking	Glasgow
7.15 p.m.	Daily	B.E.A. Dakota	Belfast
7.40 p.m.	Daily	Aer Lingus Dakota	Dublin
8.50 p.m.	Daily	Aer Lingus Dakota	Dublin
9.15 p.m.	Daily	B.E.A. Viking	Paris
10.18 p.m.	Tues., Wed., Thurs., Sat., Sun.	B.E.A. Viking	Athens
10.30 p.m.	Thurs., Sun.	Hellenic Liberator	Glasgow
11.57 p.m.	Mon., Thurs.	B.E.A. Viking	Istanbul

PRESTWICK AIRPORT (GLASGOW).

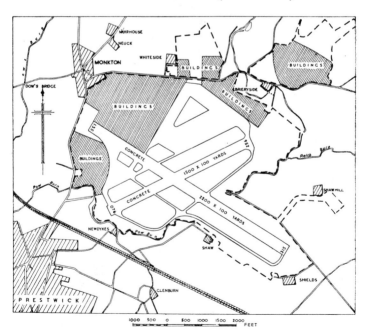

ARRIVALS.

MONDAY

Time	Aircraft	From
5.25 a.m.	K.L.M. Constellation	New York
6.40 a.m.	S.A.S. Skymaster or DC-6	New York
9.30 a.m.	K.L.M. Constellation	Curacao (West Indies)
11.20 a.m.	B.O.A.C. Liberator	Montreal
12.00 noon	B.O.A.C. Constellation	New York
3.15 p.m.	B.O.A.C. Constellation	Montreal
7.30 p.m.	C.O.B.E.T.A. Dakota	Brussels
8.10 p.m.	T.C.A. North Star	Montreal
9.45 p.m.	K.L.M. Constellation	Amsterdam
11.45 p.m.	K.L.M. Constellation	Amsterdam
11.50 p.m.	S.A.S. Skymaster or DC-6	Stockholm
12.20 midnight	S.A.S. Skymaster or DC-6	Stockholm

TUESDAY

Time	Aircraft	From
5.25 a.m.	K.L.M. Constellation	New York
6.40 a.m.	S.A.S. Skymaster or DC-6	New York
7.55 a.m.	A.O.A. Skymaster	New York
8.10 p.m.	T.C.A. North Star	Montreal
8.25 p.m.	A.O.A. Skymaster	Copenhagen
8.30 p.m.	Icelandic Liberator	Reykjavik
9.40 p.m.	Air France Languedoc 161	Paris
10.30 p.m.	S.A.S. Dakota	Oslo
10.45 p.m.	B.O.A.C. Constellation	London
11.45 p.m.	B.O.A.C. Constellation	London
11.45 p.m.	K.L.M. Constellation	Amsterdam

WEDNESDAY

Time	Aircraft	From
5.25 a.m.	K.L.M. Constellation	New York
6.40 a.m.	S.A.S. Skymaster or DC-6	New York
11.20 a.m.	B.O.A.C. Liberator	Montreal
3.15 p.m.	B.O.A.C. Constellation	Montreal
6.45 p.m.	B.O.A.C. Liberator	London
8.10 p.m.	T.C.A. North Star	Montreal
11.45 p.m.	K.L.M. Constellation	Amsterdam
12.30 midnight	S.A.S. Skymaster or DC-6	Stockholm

THURSDAY

Time	Aircraft	From
5.25 a.m.	K.L.M. Constellation	New York
6.40 a.m.	S.A.S. Skymaster or DC-6	New York
11.20 a.m.	B.O.A.C. Liberator	Montreal
12.00 noon	B.O.A.C. Constellation	New York
8.25 p.m.	A.O.A. Skymaster	Helsinki
9.40 p.m.	Air France Languedoc 161	Paris
10.30 p.m.	S.A.S. Dakota	Oslo
11.45 p.m.	B.O.A.C. Constellation	London
11.45 p.m.	K.L.M. Constellation	Amsterdam
11.50 p.m.	S.A.S. Skymaster or DC-6	Stockholm
12.20 midnight	S.A.S. Skymaster or DC-6	Stockholm

FRIDAY

Time	Aircraft	From
5.25 a.m.	K.L.M. Constellation	New York
6.40 a.m.	S.A.S. Skymaster-or DC-6	New York
9.30 a.m.	K.L.M. Constellation	Curacao (West Indies)
7.55 a.m.	A.O.A. Skymaster	New York
3.15 p.m.	B.O.A.C. Constellation	Montreal
6.45 p.m.	B.O.A.C. Liberator	London
7.30 p.m.	C.O.B.E.T.A. Dakota	Brussels
8.10 p.m.	T.C.A. North Star	Montreal
10.00 p.m.	A.O.A. Skymaster	London
10.45 p.m.	B.O.A.C. Constellation	London
11.45 p.m.	K.L.M. Constellation	Amsterdam

PRESTWICK AIRPORT—*contd.*

SATURDAY

Time	Aircraft	From
5.25 a.m.	K.L.M. Constellation	New York
6.40 a.m.	S.A.S. Skymaster or DC-6	New York·
12.00 noon	B.O.A.C. Constellation	New York
6.45 p.m.	B.O.A.C. Liberator	London
8.10 p.m.	T.C.A. North Star	Montreal
10.30 p.m.	S.A.S. Dakota	Oslo
11.45 p.m.	K.L.M. Constellation	Amsterdam
11.50 p.m.	S.A.S. Skymaster or DC-6	Stockholm
12.20 midnight	S.A.S. Skymaster or DC-6	Stockholm

SUNDAY

5.25 a.m.	K.L.M. Constellation	New York
6.30 a.m.	A.O.A. Constellation	New York
6.40 a.m.	S.A.S. Skymaster or DC-6	New York
8.10 p.m.	T.C.A. North Star	Montreal
9.05 p.m.	A.O.A. Constellation	Frankfurt
9.40 p.m.	Air France Languedoc 161	Paris
10.30 p.m.	S.A.S. Dakota	Oslo
10.45 p.m.	B.O.A.C. Constellation	London
11.45 p.m.	K.L.M. Constellation	Amsterdam

DEPARTURES.

MONDAY

Time	Aircraft	To
1.15 a.m.	K.L.M. Constellation	New York
1.20 a.m.	S.A.S. Skymaster or DC-6	New York
9.10 a.m.	S.A.S. Dakota	Oslo
9.10 a.m.	Air France Languedoc 161	Paris
11.15 a.m.	T.C.A. North Star	Montreal
5.30 p.m.	A.C.A. Skymaster	Frankfurt
11.15 p.m.	K.L.M. Constellation	Curacao (West Indies)

TUESDAY

1.15 a.m.	K.L.M. Constellation	New York
1.20 a.m.	S.A.S. Skymaster or DC-6	New York
8.00 a.m.	C.O.B.E.T.A. Dakota	Brussels
8.25 a.m.	A.O.A. Skymaster	Frankfurt
9.30 a.m.	Icelandic Liberator	Reykjavik
11.15 a.m.	T.C.A. North Star	Montreal
12.50 noon	B.O.A.C. Liberator	London
1.30 p.m.	B.O.A.C. Constellation	London
9.10 p.m.	A.O.A. Skymaster	New York
10.45 p.m.	B.O.A.C. Constellation	New York

WEDNESDAY

1.15 a.m.	K.L.M. Constellation	New York
1.20 a.m.	S.A.S. Skymaster or DC-6	New York
1.45 a.m.	B.O.A.C. Constellation	Montreal
9.10 a.m.	S.A.S. Dakota	Oslo
9.10 a.m.	Air France Languedoc 161	Paris
11.15 a.m.	T.C.A. North Star	Montreal
3.30 p.m.	Hellenic Liberator	Athens
5.30 p.m.	A.O.A. Skymaster	Frankfurt
8.15 p.m.	B.O.A.C. Liberator	Montreal

THURSDAY

1.15 a.m.	K.L.M. Constellation	New York
1.20 a.m.	S.A.S. Skymaster or DC-6	New York
11.15 a.m.	T.C.A. North Star	Montreal
12.50 noon	B.O.A.C. Liberator	London

Time	Aircraft	To
1.30 p.m.	B.O.A.C. Constellation	London
4.45 p.m.	B.O.A.C. Constellation	London
9.10 p.m.	A.O.A. Skymaster	New York
11.15 p.m.	K.L.M. Constellation	Curacao (West Indies)

FRIDAY

Time	Aircraft	To
1.15 a.m.	K.L.M. Constellation	New York
1.20 a.m.	S.A.S. Skymaster or DC-6	New York
1.45 a.m.	B.O.A.C. Constellation	Montreal
8.25 a.m.	A.O.A. Skymaster	London
9.10 a.m.	S.A.S. Dakota	Oslo
9.10 a.m.	Air France Languedoc 161	Paris
11.15 a.m.	T.C.A. North Star	Montreal
12.50 noon	B.O.A.C. Liberator	London
8.15 p.m.	B.O.A.C. Liberator	Montreal
10.30 p.m.	A.O.A. Skymaster	New York
10.45 p.m.	B.O.A.C. Constellation	New York

SATURDAY

Time	Aircraft	To
1.15 a.m.	K.L.M. Constellation	New York
1.20 a.m.	S.A.S. Skymaster or DC-6	New York
8.00 a.m.	C.O.B.E.T.A. Dakota	Brussels
11.15 a.m.	T.C.A. North Star	Montreal
3.30 p.m.	Hellenic Liberator	Athens
4.45 p.m.	B.O.A.C. Constellation	London
8.15 p.m.	B.O.A.C. Liberator	Montreal

SUNDAY

Time	Aircraft	To
1.15 a.m.	K.L.M. Constellation	New York
1.20 a.m.	S.A.S. Skymaster or DC-6	New York
1.45 a.m.	B.O.A.C. Constellation	Montreal
7.40 a.m.	A.O.A. Constellation	Frankfurt
9.10 a.m.	S.A.S. Dakota	Oslo
11.15 a.m.	T.C.A. North Star	Montreal
9.35 p.m.	A.O.A. Constellation	New York
10.45 p.m.	B.O.A.C. Constellation	New York

RENFREW AIRPORT (GLASGOW).

ARRIVALS.

Time	Frequency	Aircraft	From
8.35 a.m.	Mon., Fri., Sat.	Aer Lingus Dakota	Dublin
10.55 a.m.	Weekdays	B.E.A. Rapide	Campbeltown
11.10 a.m.	Weekdays	B.E.A. Rapide	Islay
11.13 a.m.	Weekdays	B.E.A. Viking	Northolt (London)
11.20 a.m.	Weekdays	B.E.A. Dakota	Belfast
1.05 p.m.	Daily	Aer Lingus Dakota	Dublin
3.10 p.m.	Daily	B.E.A. Dakota	Belfast
3.20 p.m.	Weekdays	B.E.A. Rapide	Campbeltown
4.05 p.m.	Weekdays	B.E.A. Dakota	Inverness
4.25 p.m.	Weekdays	B.E.A. Rapide	Benbecula
4.35 p.m.	Weekdays	B.E.A. Rapide	Tiree
4.35 p.m.	Daily	Aer Lingus Dakota	Dublin
5.13 p.m.	Weekdays	B.E.A. Viking	Northolt (London)
6.10 p.m.	Daily	B.E.A. Dakota	Belfast
7.25 p.m.	Weekdays	B.E.A. Rapide	Islay
7.30 p.m.	Weekdays	B.E.A. Dakota	Shetland
7.35 p.m.	Weekdays	B.E.A. Rapide	Campbeltown
9.10 p.m.	Weekdays	B.E.A. Dakota	Belfast
9.19 p.m.	Daily	B.E.A. Viking	Northolt (London)
10.20 p.m.	Weekdays	B.E.A. Dakota	London (via Edinburgh)

Pan American Douglas Skymaster *Clipper Gladiator* NC 88945 at London Airport.

Lockheed Constellation PP-PDA of Panair do Brasil, the Brazilian airline. The five Constellations used by Panair do Brasil on the service to London are known as the *Bandeirante* Class.

Qantas Empire Airways Constellation *Lawrence Hargrave* as operated on the London-Australia route at London Airport.   (*Photos: A. S. C. Lumsden*

(*Photo: A. S. C. Lumsden*

South African Airways Douglas DC-4 Skymaster ZS-BMF *Amatola* at London Airport. S.A.A. employ seven Skymasters on the Johannesburg-London route. The company name appears on the port side of the fuselage in Afrikaans and on the starboard side in English.

(*Photo: Sabena*

A Douglas DC-6 of the Belgian airline company S.A.B.E.N.A. Belgian DC-6 aircraft call at Shannon Airport on the route from Brussels to New York.

(*Photo: A. S. C. Lumsden*

Douglas DC-3 Dakota OO-AUQ, as used by S.A.B.E.N.A. on the services from London Airport to Antwerp and Brussels.

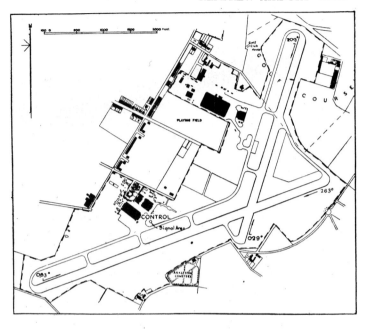

DEPARTURES.

Time	Frequency	Aircraft	To
8.10 a.m.	Weekdays	B.E.A. Dakota	Inverness
8.30 a.m.	Weekdays	B.E.A. Dakota	Belfast
8.35 a.m.	Weekdays	B.E.A. Dakota	London (via Edinburgh)
8.58 a.m.	Weekdays	B.E.A. Viking	Northolt (London)
9.05 a.m.	Weekdays	B.E.A. Rapide	Islay
9.20 a.m.	Weekdays	B.E.A. Rapide	Campbeltown
9.25 a.m.	Weekdays	B.E.A. Rapide	Benbecula
9.52 a.m.	Sunday	B.E.A. Viking	Northolt (London)
11.55 a.m.	Daily	B.E.A. Dakota	Belfast
11.58 a.m.	Weekdays	B.E.A. Viking	Northolt (London)
12.00 noon	Weekdays	B.E.A. Dakota	Shetland
1.35 p.m.	Daily	Aer Lingus Dakota	Dublin
1.45 p.m.	Weekdays	B.E.A. Rapide	Campbeltown
2.05 p.m.	Weekdays	B.E.A. Rapide	Tiree
3.40 p.m.	Daily	B.E.A. Dakota	Belfast
5.05 p.m.	Daily	Aer Lingus Dakota	Dublin
5.15 p.m.	Weekdays	B.E.A. Rapide	Islay
6.00 p.m.	Weekdays	B.E.A. Rapide	Campbeltown
6.28 p.m.	Weekdays	B.E.A. Viking	Northolt (London)
6.05 p.m.	Mon., Fri.	Aer Lingus, Dakota	Dublin
6.40 p.m.	Weekdays	B.E.A. Dakota	Belfast
9.05 p.m.	Mon., Fri., Sat.	Aer Lingus Dakota	Dublin

RONALDSWAY AIRPORT (ISLE OF MAN).

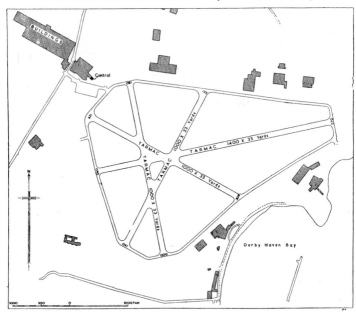

ARRIVALS.

Time	Frequency	Aircraft	From
8.50 a.m.	Weekdays	B.E.A. Dakota	Liverpool
9.10 a.m.	Daily	B.E.A. Dakota	Manchester
9.55 a.m.	Weekdays	B.E.A. Dakota	Renfrew (Glasgow)
10.05 a.m.	Daily	B.E.A. Dakota	Liverpool
10.55 a.m.	Sunday	B.E.A. Dakota	Renfrew (Glasgow)
12.40 noon	Daily	B.E.A. Dakota	Liverpool
1.46 p.m.	Daily	B.E.A. Dakota	Northolt (London)
2.30 p.m.	Sunday	B.E.A. Dakota	Renfrew (Glasgow)
3.10 p.m.	Daily	B.E.A. Dakota	Blackpool
3.35 p.m.	Daily	B.E.A. Dakota	Manchester
4.20 p.m.	Daily	B.E.A. Dakota	Liverpool
5.30 p.m.	Daily	B.E.A. Dakota	Renfrew (Glasgow)
5.55 p.m.	Daily	B.E.A. Dakota	Liverpool
7.45 p.m.	Daily	B.E.A. Dakota	Blackpool
8.25 p.m.	Mon., Fri., Sat., Sun.	B.E.A. Dakota	Liverpool
9.30 p.m.	Daily	B.E.A. Dakota	Liverpool

DEPARTURES.

Time	Frequency	Aircraft	To
8.00 a.m.	Weekdays	B.E.A. Dakota	Liverpool
9.05 a.m.	Weekdays	B.E.A. Dakota	Belfast
9.30 a.m.	Daily	B.E.A. Dakota	Manchester
10.25 a.m.	Weekdays	B.E.A. Dakota	Renfrew (Glasgow)
10.35 a.m.	Daily	B.E.A. Dakota	Liverpool
11.30 a.m.	Sunday	B.E.A. Dakota	Renfrew (Glasgow)
1.25 p.m.	Daily	B.E.A. Dakota	Blackpool

Time	Frequency	Aircraft	To
2.15 p.m.	Daily	B.E.A. Dakota	Liverpool
3.00 p.m.	Sunday	B.E.A. Dakota	Renfrew (Glasgow)
4.00 p.m.	Daily	B.E.A. Dakota	Liverpool
4.15 p.m.	Daily	B.E.A. Dakota	Manchester
6.00 p.m.	Daily	B.E.A. Dakota	Blackpool
6.25 p.m.	Mon., Fri., Sat., Sun.	B.E.A. Dakota	Liverpool
7.15 p.m.	Daily	B.E.A. Dakota	Liverpool
8.30 p.m.	Daily	B.E.A. Dakota	Renfrew (Glasgow)
8.45 p.m.	Daily	B.E.A. Dakota	Liverpool

SHANNON AIRPORT

ARRIVALS.

Time	Frequency	Aircraft	From
00.05 a.m.	Fri., Sun.	T.C.A. North Star	London
00.15 a.m.	Saturday	A.O.A. Skymaster	London
00.20 a.m.	Wednesday	A.O.A. Skymaster	Frankfurt
00.20 a.m.	Mon., Fri., Sun.	A.O.A. Skymaster	Berlin
00.30 a.m.	Alternate Fridays	Swissair Skymaster	Geneva
00.45 a.m.	Mon., Wed., Sat.	Sabena DC-6	Brussels
1.50 a.m.	Tues., Fri.	Air France Constellation	New York
2.50 a.m.	Monday	Air France Constellation	Paris
4.20 a.m.	Friday	A.O.A. Constellation	New York
4.30 a.m.	Wednesday	A.O.A. Constellation	Washington
4.30 a.m.	Mon., Thurs., Sun.	A.O.A. Constellation	New York
5.30 a.m.	Weekdays	A.O.A. Skymaster	New York
5.55 a.m.	Saturday	T.W.A. Constellation or DC-4	Cairo
6.25 a.m.	Mon., Wed., Fri.	T.W.A. Skymaster	Cairo
6.50 a.m.	Mon., Wed., Thurs.	Air France Constellation	New York
9.00 a.m.	Alternate Mondays	Swissair Skymaster	New York
9.15 a.m.	Weekdays	P.A.A. Skymaster	New York
9.30 a.m.	Mon., Tues.	P.A.A. Skymaster	New York
10.25 a.m.	Wednesday	T.W.A. Skymaster Freighter	Cairo
11.00 a.m.	Daily	P.A.A. Constellation	New York
11.30 a.m.	Mon., Wed., Sat.	B.O.A.C. Constellation	New York
12.50 noon	Thursday	Air France Constellation	New York
1.00 p.m.	Wed., Fri.	T.C.A. North Star	Montreal
2.10 p.m.	Sunday	T.W.A. Skymaster Freighter	Washington
3.15 p.m.	Saturday	T.W.A. Constellation	New York
4.50 p.m.	Daily	Aer Lingus Dakota	London
6.20 p.m.	Mon., Tues.	T.W.A. Constellation	Bombay
7.00 p.m.	Sunday	P.A.A. Skymaster Freighter	New York
7.15 p.m.	Tues, Wed., Thurs., Fri., Sat., Sun.	P.A.A. Skymaster	Munich
8.25 p.m.	Mon., Wed., Fri., Sun.	A.O.A. Constellation	London
8.25 p.m.	Sunday	T.W.A. Constellation or DC-4	Chicago
8.35 p.m.	Friday	T.W.A. Constellation	Bombay
8.40 p.m.	Mon., Wed., Thurs., Fri.	T.W.A. Constellation	New York
9.00 p.m.	Mon., Wed., Sat.	B.O.A.C. Constellation	London
9.35 p.m.	Thursday	A.O.A. Constellation	Frankfurt
9.45 p.m.	Tuesday	T.W.A. Constellation	Washington
9.50 p.m.	Daily	Aer Lingus Dakota	Dublin
10.00 p.m.	Wednesday	P.A.A. Skymaster	London
10.45 p.m.	Mon., Fri.	A.O.A. Constellation	Frankfurt
10.50 p.m.	Daily	P.A.A. Constellation	London
11.05 p.m.	Sunday	A.O.A. Constellation	Frankfurt
11.50 p.m.	Weekdays	Air France Constellation	Paris

DEPARTURES.

Time	Frequency	Aircraft	To
00.05 a.m.	Daily	P.A.A. Constellation	New York
00.05 a.m.	Monday	A.O.A. Constellation	New York
1.05 a.m.	Fri., Sun.	T.C.A. North Star	Montreal
1.20 a.m.	Tues., Wed., Thurs., Sat., Sun.	Air France Constellation	New York
1.20 a.m.	Mon., Wed., Fri., Sun.	A.O.A. Skymaster	New York
1.45 a.m.	Saturday	A.O.A. Skymaster	New York
2.00 a.m.	Alternate Fridays	Swissair Skymaster	New York
2.15 a.m.	Mon., Wed., Sat.	Sabena DC-6	New York
4.20 a.m.	Monday	Air France Constellation	New York
4.50 a.m.	Friday	A.O.A. Constellation	Frankfurt
5.00 a.m.	Mon., Wed.	A.O.A. Constellation	Frankfurt
5.05 a.m.	Thurs., Sun.	A.O.A. Constellation	Frankfurt
6.00 a.m.	Mon., Thurs., Sat.	A.O.A. Skymaster	Berlin
6.15 a.m.	Tuesday	A.O.A. Skymaster	Frankfurt
6.15 a.m.	Friday	A.O.A. Skymaster	London
7.55 a.m.	Monday	T.W.A. Constellation	New York
7.55 a.m.	Wednesday	T.W.A. Constellation or DC-4	Chicago
7.55 a.m.	Friday	T.W.A. Constellation or DC-4	Washington
8.05 a.m.	Wed., Fri., Sun.	T.W.A. Skymaster	Paris
8.20 a.m.	Mon., Wed., Fri.	Air France Constellation	Paris
10.00 a.m.	Mon., Tues.	A.O.A. Skymaster	Stockholm
10.00 a.m.	Alternate Mondays	Swissair Skymaster	Geneva
10.20 a.m.	Tues., Fri.	Air France Constellation	Paris
10.25 a.m.	Wednesday	T.W.A. Skymaster Freighter	New York
10.30 a.m.	Weekdays	P.A.A. Skymaster	Prague
10.30 a.m.	Daily	Aer Lingus Dakota	London
11.10 a.m.	Thursday	T.W.A. Skymaster	Paris
12.15 noon	Daily	P.A.A. Constellation	London
12.15 noon	Monday	T.W.A. Skymaster	Paris
12.45 noon	Mon., Wed., Sat.	B.O.A.C. Constellation	London
1.00 p.m.	Thursday	P.A.A. Skymaster	New York
2.00 p.m.	Wed., Fri.	T.C.A. North Star	London
2.20 p.m.	Thursday	Air France Constellation	Paris
3.10 p.m.	Sunday	T.W.A. Constellation or DC-4	Cairo
4.15 p.m.	Saturday	T.W.A. Constellation or DC-4	Cairo
5.45 p.m.	Daily	Aer Lingus Dakota	Dublin
5.55 p.m.	Saturday	T.W.A. Constellation	New York
6.20 p.m.	Tuesday	T.W.A. Constellation	New York
7.50 p.m.	Monday	T.W.A. Constellation or DC-4	New York
8.00 p.m.	Sunday	P.A.A. Skymaster	Brussels
8.30 p.m.	Tues., Wed., Thurs., Fri., Sat., Sun.	P.A.A. Skymaster	New York
9.25 p.m.	Sunday	T.W.A. Skymaster	Cairo
9.25 p.m.	Mon., Wed., Fri.	A.O.A. Constellation	New York
9.25 p.m.	Sunday	A.O.A. Constellation	Washington
9.40 p.m.	Mon., Fri., Thurs.	T.W.A. Constellation	Bombay
9.40 p.m.	Wednesday	T.W.A. Skymaster	Cairo
10.05 p.m.	Friday	T.W.A. Constellation or DC-4	New York
10.35 p.m.	Thursday	A.O.A. Constellation	New York
10.45 p.m.	Mon., Wed., Sat.	B.O.A.C. Constellation	New York
10.45 p.m.	Tuesday	T.W.A. Skymaster	Cairo
11.45 p.m.	Mon., Wed., Fri.	A.O.A. Constellation	New York

EASTLEIGH AIRPORT (SOUTHAMPTON).

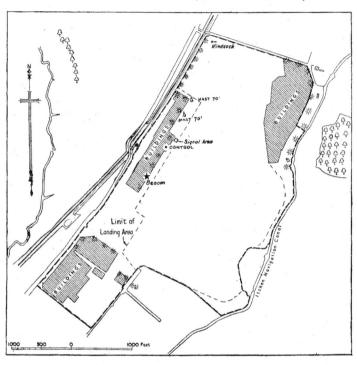

ARRIVALS.

Time	Frequency	Aircraft	From
10.50 a.m.	Daily	B.E.A. Dakota	Jersey
11.40 a.m.	Daily	B.E.A. Rapide	Jersey
12.55 noon	Daily	B.E.A. Dakota	Guernsey
1.55 p.m.	Daily	B.E.A. Dakota	Jersey
3.10 p.m.	Mon., Fri., Sat., Sun.	B.E.A. Rapide	Jersey
5.30 p.m.	Daily	B.E.A. Dakota	Jersey

DEPARTURES.

Time	Frequency	Aircraft	To
11.25 a.m.	Daily	B.E.A. Dakota	Jersey
11.55 a.m.	Daily	B.E.A. Rapide	Jersey
1.25 p.m.	Daily	B.E.A. Dakota	Guernsey
2.25 p.m.	Daily	B.E.A. Dakota	Jersey
3.30 p.m.	Mon., Fri., Sat., Sun.	B.E.A. Rapide	Jersey
6.00 p.m.	Daily	B.E.A. Dakota	Jersey

MARINE AIR TERMINAL, BERTH 50, SOUTHAMPTON.

ARRIVALS.

MONDAY
3.00 p.m.   B.O.A.C. " Plymouth " Class from Hong-Kong

WEDNESDAY
1.00 p.m.   B.O.A.C. " Hythe " Class from Karachi
3.30 p.m.   B.O.A.C. " Hythe " Class from Australia

THURSDAY
3.00 p.m.   B.O.A.C. " Plymouth " Class from Tokyo
3.30 p.m.   B.O.A.C. Solent from Johannesburg

FRIDAY
3.30 p.m.   B.O.A.C. " Hythe " Class from Australia

SATURDAY
3.30 p.m.   B.O.A.C. Solent from Johannesburg

SUNDAY
3.30 p.m.   B.O.A.C. " Hythe " Class from Australia
3.30 p.m.   B.O.A.C. Solent from Johannesburg

DEPARTURES.

MONDAY
11.45 a.m.   B.O.A.C. " Hythe " Class to Australia

TUESDAY
11.45 a.m.   B.O.A.C. Solent to Johannesburg
12.30 a.m.   B.O.A.C. " Plymouth " Class to Hong-Kong

WEDNESDAY
11.45 a.m.   B.O.A.C. " Hythe " Class to Australia

THURSDAY
11.45 a.m.   B.O.A.C. " Hythe " Class to Karachi

FRIDAY
11.45 a.m.   B.O.A.C. Solent to Johannesburg
12.30 p.m.   B.O.A.C. " Plymouth " Class to Tokyo

SATURDAY
11.45 a.m.   B.O.A.C. " Hythe " Class to Australia

SUNDAY
11.45 a.m.   B.O.A.C. Solent to Johannesburg

AIRLINERS IN REGULAR SERVICE
— SILHOUETTES & DETAILS —

AIRSPEED CONSUL.

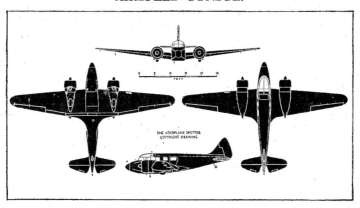

THE AEROPLANE SPOTTER
COPYRIGHT DRAWING

General Description.	Twin-engine low-wing monoplane with single fin and rudder, constructed by Airspeed Ltd., at Portsmouth.
Seating Capacity.	Crew of two and five passengers.
Engines.	Two Armstrong-Siddeley Cheetah X, each of 395 h.p.
Dimensions.	Span : 53 ft. 4 ins. Length : 35 ft. 4 ins.
Performance.	Cruising speed : 150 m.p.h. Range : 900 miles.

First built in 1945, the Consul is a civil conversion of the R.A.F. Oxford navigation trainer, of which nearly 10,000 were built during the war. As the Oxford was in turn derived from the civil Envoy of 1934, the basic design conception of the Consul is thus at least fifteen years old. Production commenced in March, 1946, and the Consul is now one of the most widely-used aircraft in service with charter companies. There are about one hundred Consuls in commercial operation in Britain alone and many more overseas.

AVRO XIX ANSON.

General Description.	Twin-engine low-wing monoplane with single fin and rudder, constructed by A. V. Roe & Co. Ltd. at Yeadon and Manchester.
Seating Capacity.	Crew of two and six or nine passengers.
Engines.	Two Armstrong-Siddeley Cheetah XV, each of 420 h.p.
Dimensions.	Span : 56 ft. 6 ins. Length : 42 ft. 3 ins.
Performance.	Cruising speed : 155 m.p.h. Range : 570 miles.

The Anson has had a very long career and there are several variations of the basic design in service with the charter companies. Some are

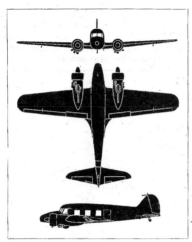

AVRO XIX ANSON—*contd.*

converted ex-R.A.F. trainers, but the majority are of the Avro XIX type which was produced as a civil version of the military Anson XII in 1944. Like the Consul, the Avro XIX derives from a military aircraft which was initially developed itself from a civil design. Military service of the Anson dates back to 1936, and the civil machine from which it was developed was the Avro 652, two of which served with the old Imperial Airways from 1934 onwards. Fundamentally unchanged in outline since 1934, the latest Anson differs in having a tapered all-metal wing.

AVRO LANCASTRIAN.

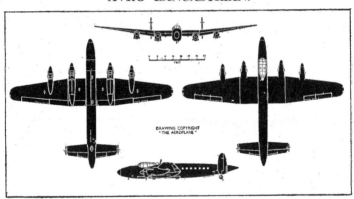

General Description.	Four-engine mid-wing monoplane with twin fins and rudders, constructed by A. V. Roe & Co. Ltd., at Manchester.
Seating Capacity.	Crew of five and thirteen passengers.
Engines.	Four Rolls-Royce Merlin T.24, each of 1,640 h.p.
Dimensions.	Span : 102 ft. 0 ins. Length : 76 ft. 10 ins.
Performance.	Cruising speed : 280 m.p.h. Range : 2,820 miles. With 13 passengers.

One of the several British airliner types derived from war-time bombers for the immediate post-war period, the Lancastrian is a civil version of the renowned Lancaster bomber. First manufactured and used commercially in Canada during 1943, production in Britain for both the R.A.F. and B.O.A.C. began in 1944. Lancastrians pioneered post-war landplane routes to Australia with B.O.A.C. and to South America with B.S.A.A.C. The Lancastrian can boast high speed but restricted cabin capacity reduces its value for commercial operation and it is now being relegated to freighter duties as newer types come into service.

AVRO TUDOR IV.

General Description. Four-engine low-wing monoplane with single fin and rudder, constructed by A. V. Roe & Co. Ltd., at Manchester.

Seating Capacity. Crew of four and thirty-two passengers.

Engines. Four Rolls-Royce Merlin 621, each of 1,752 h.p.

Dimensions. Span : 120 ft. 0 ins. Length : 85 ft. 6 ins.

Performance. Cruising speed : 280 m.p.h. Range : 3,700 miles.

First of the Tudor series to go into regular airline operation, the Tudor IV was grounded by the Ministry of Civil Aviation early in 1948 owing to the unfortunate loss of *Star Tiger* over the South Atlantic. The type is now in operation again, but is provisionally restricted to freight work. Much controversy rages over the technical aspects of this matter, but it is fairly safe to say that the Tudor IV is a promising aircraft and that the temporary withdrawal was merely a reflection of extreme caution. The original Tudor, designed for transatlantic operation, first flew in 1945.

AVRO YORK.

General Description. Four-engine high-wing monoplane with three fins. Constructed by A. V. Roe & Co. Ltd., at Manchester

Seating Capacity. Crew of four and twenty-four passengers.

Engines. Four Rolls-Royce Merlin T.24, each of 1,640 h.p.

Dimensions. Span: 102 ft. 0 ins. Length : 78 ft. 0 ins.

Performance. Cruising speed : 260 m.p.h. Range : 2,700 miles.

Utilizing many Lancaster components to facilitate production, the York was developed in 1942 as a military transport for the R.A.F., the first machine flying in July, 1942. Yorks became the personal transports of a number of high-ranking personages, including Mr. Winston Churchill

AVRO YORK—*contd.*

and Field-Marshal Smuts. Yorks for civil use were in service before the war ended, B.O.A.C. taking delivery of their first York early in 1944. Still a mainstay of B.O.A.C. equipment, the York is also in service with British South American Airways, Skyways Ltd. and the Argentine company F.A.M.A. Production of the York finally ceased in April, 1948.

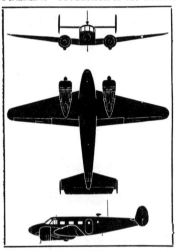

BEECH EXPEDITER.

General Description. Twin-engine low-wing monoplane with twin fins and rudders. Constructed by the Beech Aircraft Corporation, Wichita, Kansas, U.S.A.

Seating Capacity. Crew of two and six passengers.

Engines. Two Pratt and Whitney Wasp Junior, each of 450 h.p.

Dimensions. Span : 47 ft. 8 ins. Length : 34 ft. 3 ins.

Performance. Cruising speed : 220 m.p.h. Range : 900 miles.

Used extensively by the French charter company *Air Transport* on its services to Croydon and Gatwick, the Beech Expediter is a type formerly used by the United States Air Force in Europe during the war. Surplus Beech aircraft have been sold to a number of European airline companies. The Expediter is in much the same category as the British Anson and Consul, but has a rather higher performance. The original version of the Expediter was first flown in 1937.

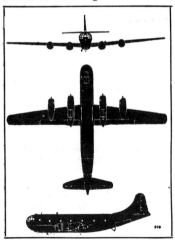

BOEING STRATOCRUISER.

General Description. Four-engine mid-wing monoplane with single fin and rudder. Constructed by the Boeing Airplane Company, Seattle, Washington, U.S.A.

Seating Capacity. Crew of five and maximum passenger accommodation for one hundred.

Engines. Four Pratt and Whitney Wasp Major, each of 3,500 h.p.

Dimensions. Span : 141 ft. 3 ins. Length 110 ft. 4 ins.

Performance. Cruising speed : 300 m.p.h. Range : 4,100 miles.

Developed concurrently with the Stratofreighter, a similar aircraft for the United States Air Force, the Stratocruiser is nearing the end of its acceptance trials and deliveries to airlines are expected to commence before the end of 1948. Just as the British Tudor airliners employ the same wing design as the Lincoln bomber, so does the Stratocruiser incorporate the same wings as the Superfortress bomber. B.O.A.C. has five Stratocruisers on order to supplement the Constellations on the London-New York route.

BRISTOL FREIGHTER AND WAYFARER.

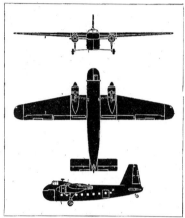

General Description. Twin-engine high-wing monoplane with single fin and rudder and non-retracting under-carriage. Constructed by the Bristol Aeroplane Company Ltd., Filton, Bristol.

Seating Capacity Crew of two and (Wayfarer). thirty-six passengers.

Engines. Two Bristol Hercules 638, each of 1,690 h.p.

Dimensions. Span: 108 ft. 0 ins. Length : 68 ft. 4 ins.

Performance. Cruising speed : 170 m.p.h. Range : 1,100 miles.

The Bristol Type 170 Freighter was originally intended as a troop transport for service in the Far East, but with the end of the war it was decided to place the aircraft on the civil market as a short-haul high-capacity passenger or freight-carrying machine. The passenger version is known as the Wayfarer and both versions are similar externally. Freighters and Wayfarers have sold well in the export market and, amongst the foreign airlines, the French firm Air Transport operates Wayfarers into Gatwick. The latest model of the Freighter has rounded wing-tips, the earlier version having square-cut wings of rather less span.

CANADAIR DC-4M NORTH STAR.

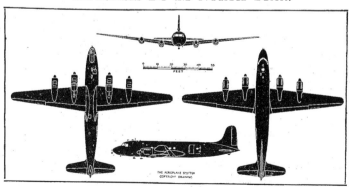

CANADAIR DC-4M—*contd.*

General Description.	Four-engine low-wing monoplane with single fin and rudder. Constructed by Canadair Ltd., Montreal, Canada.
Seating Capacity.	Crew of four and twenty-four passengers.
Engines.	Four Rolls-Royce Merlin 620, each of 1,780 h.p.
Dimensions.	Span : 117 ft. 6 ins. Length : 93 ft. 5 ins.
Performance.	Cruising speed : 319 m.p.h. Range : 3,065 miles.

Essentially a Douglas DC-4 built under licence in Canada, the Canadair DC-4M differs from its American counterpart in having Rolls-Royce Merlin engines in place of the Twin Wasp radials. First produced in 1943 to meet the requirements of Trans-Canada Airlines, the DC-4M, popularly known as the North Star, incorporates many refinements over the original DC-4, and has many features of the later DC-6. The first six DC-4M aircraft did not have the fully-pressurized passenger cabin of the twenty DC-4M2 versions now in service. B.O.A.C. is to purchase twenty-two DC-4M4 airliners for service on the N. Atlantic and Middle East routes.

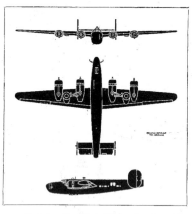

CONSOLIDATED LIBERATOR.

General Description. Four-engine high-wing monoplane with twin fins and rudders. Constructed by the Consolidated-Vultee Aircraft Corporation, San Diego, California, U.S.A.

Seating Capacity. Varies with requirements of operator.

Engines. Four Pratt and Whitney Twin Wasp, each of 1,200 h.p.

Dimensions. Span : 110 ft. 0 ins. Length : 66 ft. 4 ins.

Performance. Cruising speed : 220 m.p.h. Range : 2,500 miles.

In company with the Flying Fortress, the Liberator was the standard heavy bomber of the U.S. Air Force during the war and some were also supplied to the R.A.F. under Lend-Lease. A capacious fuselage and exceptional range made the Liberator especially suitable for transport duties and the original machines supplied to the R.A.F. in 1941 were converted for this work. Liberators gave good service on the war-time routes of B.O.A.C., but the type is now obsolescent and carries only freight on the Atlantic services, although Scottish Airlines and its subsidiary Hellenic Airways still use the passenger version. Recently, B.O.A.C. Liberators have been employed on flight refuelling experiments. The original Liberator flew in 1939.

CONVAIR 240.

General Description.	Twin-engine low-wing monoplane with single fin and rudder Constructed by the Consolidated-Vultee Corporation, San Diego California, U.S.A.

CONVAIR 240—*contd.*

Seating Capacity. Crew of four and forty passengers.

Engines. Two Pratt and Whitney Double Wasp, each of 2,400 h.p.

Dimensions. Span: 91 ft. 9 ins. Length : 74 ft. 8 ins.

Performance. Cruising speed : 300 m.p.h. Range : 800 miles.

The American equivalent in performance and capacity of the British Airspeed Ambassador, the Convair 240 is the modern replacement for the evergreen Dakota. Convair Liners are scheduled to replace Dakotas on the European routes of S.A.B.E.N.A., K.L.M. and Swissair. The Convair 240 made its maiden flight in March, 1947, and over 150 are now being built for airlines in the U.S.A., Latin America and Australia, as well as the European companies previously mentioned.

DE HAVILLAND DOVE.

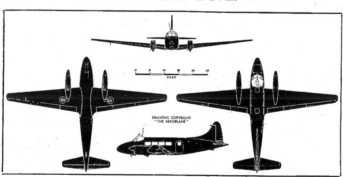

General Description. Twin-engine low-wing monoplane with single fin and rudder. Constructed by the De Havilland Aircraft Company Ltd., Hatfield, Herts.

Seating Capacity. Crew of two and eight passengers.

Engines. Two D.H. Gipsy Queen 70, each of 340 h.p.

Dimensions. Span : 57 ft. 0 ins. Length : 39 ft. 6 ins.

Performance. Cruising speed : 179 m.p.h. Range : 780 miles.

Enjoying a most healthy sale in the export market, the Dove is a wholly

DE HAVILLAND DOVE—*contd.*

post-war production and continues the De Havilland tradition of success in the light transport field which was established by the Dragon and Dragon Rapide biplanes. Succeeding the Rapide as a light transport and feeder liner with low operating and maintenance costs, the Dove shares with the Miles Aerovan the introduction of the tricycle undercarriage in standard British transport aircraft. Heavier British airliners currently in service employ the older form of tailwheel undercarriage long since abandoned by the American transports. The first Dove flew in September, 1945. A pleasant feature of the Dove is the excellent vision from the passengers' cabin provided by the large windows.

DE HAVILLAND DRAGON RAPIDE.

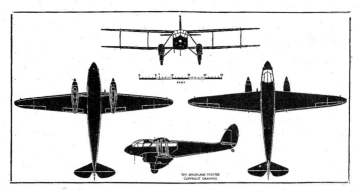

General Description.	Twin-engine biplane with tapered wings, fixed undercarriage and single fin and rudder. Constructed by De Havilland Aircraft Company Ltd., Witney, Oxford, and Brush Coachwork Ltd., Loughborough, Leicester.
Seating Capacity.	Crew of two and six passengers or crew of one and eight passengers.
Engines.	Two D.H. Gipsy Queen III, each of 200 h.p.
Dimensions.	Span : 48 ft. 0 ins. Length : 34 ft. 6 ins.
Performance.	Cruising speed : 123 m.p.h. Range : 495 miles.

Undoubtedly the most popular light airliner ever produced, the economical operating costs of the Dragon Rapide made it the mainstay of internal air routes in the United Kingdom before the war, and indeed made many such routes otherwise impracticable a commercial proposition. Nearly 700 Rapides were built between 1934 and 1946, the type being used during the war as the Dominie wireless and navigation trainer. Now converted once more for civil operation, the Rapide forms part of the fleet of nearly every charter operator in Great Britain. Its ability to operate from small grass aerodromes makes it especially suitable for operation in the Scottish islands, where it is mainly used by British European Airways.

One of the fleet of 17 Douglas DC-6 airliners recently placed into operation by S.A.S., and now used on the Copenhagen-Stockholm to London Northolt) route.

Scandinavian Airlines System Vickers Viking *Tormund Viking* OY-DLO. S.A.S. Vikings share the Copenhagen-London route with DC-6s.

(Photos: A. S. C. Lumsden

Douglas Dakota SE-BAS of A.B.A. (Swedish Airlines) at Northolt.

Upper: Swissair Douglas DC-4 Skymaster HB-ILA at Northolt Airport.
Lower: A Douglas DC-3 Dakota of Swissair at Northolt. Swissair's
Dakotas are scheduled for replacement by Convair 240 Liners.

(Photos: A. S. C. Lumsden

Upper: One of the twenty Canadair North Star II airliners employed on
the transatlantic route and home transcontinental routes by Trans-
Canada Airlines.
Lower: Lockheed Constellation NC 86505 *Paris Sky Chief* of Trans-
World Airline at Shannon Airport. Sabena DC-6s and Air France
Constellations also operate through Shannon.

DOUGLAS DC.-3 DAKOTA.

General Description.	Twin-engine low-wing monoplane with single fin and rudder. Constructed by the Douglas Aircraft Company, Santa Monica, California, U.S.A.
Seating Capacity.	Crew of three and from fourteen to twenty-one passengers.
Engines.	Two Pratt and Whitney Twin Wasp, each of 1,200 h.p.
Dimensions.	Span : 95 ft. 0 ins. Length : 64 ft. 5 ins.
Performance.	Cruising speed : 185 m.p.h. Range : 1,500 miles.

Most widely known of all transport aircraft, the Douglas DC-3 was christened the Dakota by the R.A.F. during the war and the name has been retained by the post-war civil airliner conversions. Although first introduced as early as 1936 for American domestic airlines, the DC-3 is to-day the most widely-used airliner type in the world and will probably remain so until at least 1950. Produced in vast quantities during the war for service as a troop-carrier with every Allied air force, there were as a result many surplus Dakotas available for conversion to civil standard with the arrival of peace and these aircraft were eagerly snapped up by those European airline companies which had lost their original fleet due to war action. The popular impression created by the lay press that the Dakota is an accident-prone aircraft is completely fallacious. As the Dakota is used by very nearly every airline in the world, it is obvious that when accidents on regular routes do occur it is frequently a Dakota which is involved. The law of averages would produce similar statistics for any aircraft so widely used as the Dakota.

DOUGLAS DC-4 SKYMASTER.

General Description.	Four-engine low-wing monoplane with single fin and rudder. Constructed by the Douglas Aircraft Company, Santa Monica, California, U.S.A.
Seating Capacity.	Crew of five and forty-four passengers or twenty-two sleeping berths.
Engines.	Four Pratt and Whitney Twin Wasp, each of 1,350 h.p.
Dimensions.	Span : 117 ft. 6 ins. Length : 93 ft. 11 ins.
Performance.	Cruising speed : 239 m.p.h. Range : 3,300 miles.

DOUGLAS DC-4 SKYMASTER—*contd.*

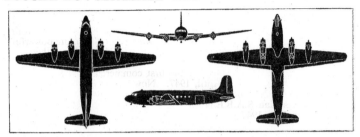

The original DC-4 of 1939 differed considerably from the form in which we now know it as the Skymaster, the early version being larger, with triple fins and rudders. The present model with the single fin first flew in April, 1942, and although originally intended for American domestic airlines the entry of U.S.A. in the war saw the DC-4 taken over by the Army as a troop transport. Consequently, the Skymaster did not see service as a civil airliner until 1945 when Skymasters declared surplus by the U.S. Army were stripped of military equipment and refurnished for service on trunk routes with American, Belgian, Dutch, French and Swedish airlines. Skymasters have been converted to civil requirements by the Glenn Martin and Republic aircraft factories.

DOUGLAS DC-6.

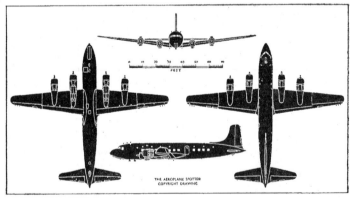

General Description.	Four-engine low-wing monoplane with single fin and rudder. Constructed by the Douglas Aircraft Company, Santa Monica, California, U.S.A.
Seating Capacity.	Crew of six and fifty-two passengers or twenty-six sleeper berths.
Engines.	Four Pratt and Whitney Double Wasp, each of 1,700 h.p.
Dimensions.	Span : 117 ft. 6 ins. Length : 100 ft. 7 ins.
Performance.	Cruising speed : 300 m.p.h. Range : 4,480 miles.

The DC-6 is the latest of the famous Douglas series of airliners in service on world air routes and is a direct development of the DC-4, from which it differs in having a longer, more capacious fuselage, more powerful engines and a cabin pressurized for operation to 19,000 ft. Otherwise the DC-6 and the earlier DC-4 are outwardly similar. The original DC-6 flew in February, 1946, and the first commercial flight was by a United Airlines machine in April, 1947. Now in service with a number of European airlines, including K.L.M. and the Scandinavian Airlines System, the Belgian S.A.B.E.N.A. firm took delivery of the first DC-6 in Europe in July, 1947.

LANGUEDOC 161.

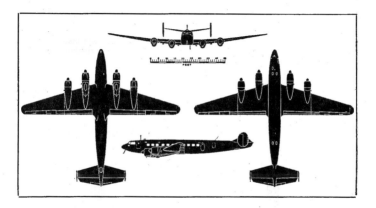

General Description.	Four-engine low-wing monoplane with twin fins and rudders. Constructed by Societe Nationale de Constructions Aeronautiques de Sud-Est, Paris, France.
Seating Capacity.	Crew of five and thirty-three passengers.
Engines.	Four Gnome-Rhone 14N, each of 1,200 h.p.
Dimensions.	Span : 96 ft. 5 ins. Length : 79 ft. 7 ins.
Performance.	Cruising speed : 233 m.p.h. Range : 1.700 miles.

Major type of airliner employed on the European network of Air France, including the London-Paris service, the Languedoc 161 was originally designed as the S.O. (Bloch) 161, a development of the Bloch 160 of 1938, and the first machine flew at Bordeaux in 1939. Outbreak of war delayed further progress and the prototype aircraft, later confiscated by the Germans, did not complete its flight trials until January, 1942. Manufacture of the Languedoc 161 in quantity did not commence until after the liberation of France when the re-constituted Air France ordered forty. The first post-war production aircraft flew in September, 1945 and deliveries to Air France are now completed.

LOCKHEED CONSTELLATION.

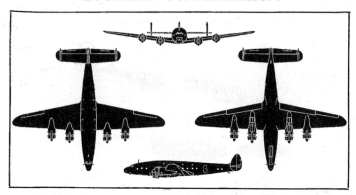

General Description.	Four-engine low-wing monoplane with triple fins and rudders. Constructed by the Lockheed Aircraft Corporation, Burbank, California, U.S.A.
Seating Capacity.	Crew of five and forty-eight passengers or twenty-two sleeper berths.
Engines.	Four Wright Duplex Cyclone, each of 2,500 h.p.
Dimensions.	Span : 123 ft. 0 ins. Length 95 ft. 1 in.
Performance.	Cruising speed : 321 m.p.h. Range : 4,630 miles.

Now the most widely-used type of airliner on the transatlantic route from London to New York, the aesthetically satisfying lines of the Constellation are a common sight at London Airport where " Connies " of B.O.A.C., Pan American and American Overseas Airlines are daily visitors. The Constellation is also used on the North Atlantic crossing by T.W.A. and Air France, operating through Shannon Airport, and by K.L.M. through Prestwick. In the same way as the Skymaster, the Constellation was designed initially for American domestic airlines but overtaken by war and commandeered by the U.S. Air Force. The first Constellation flew in January, 1943. Fifty Constellations laid down for the U.S. Air Force were converted as civil airliners when the war ended and delivered to commercial operators in 1946 as the Model 49. Latest production version, outwardly similar, has additional petrol tanks in the wings and various other refinements and is known as the Model 749.

MILES AEROVAN.

General Description.	Twin-engine high-wing monoplane with triple fins and rudders, tadpole fuselage and tricycle undercarriage. Constructed by Miles Aircraft Ltd. at Reading, Berks.
Seating Capacity.	Crew of one and nine passengers.
Engines.	Two Blackburn Cirrus Major III, each of 155 h.p.
Dimensions.	Span : 50 ft. 0 ins. Length : 34 ft. 4 ins.
Performance.	Cruising speed : 112 m.p.h. Range : 400 miles.

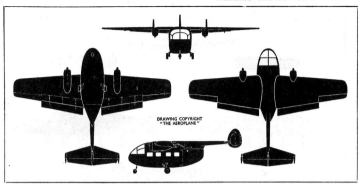

DRAWING COPYRIGHT "THE AEROPLANE"

A useful " maid-of-all-work " primarily used by charter companies, the Aerovan serves both as a short-haul passenger aircraft for local services or as a freighter carrying a variety of cargoes, ranging from light cars and race horses to crates of fruit and furniture. Freight is loaded through the hinged rear door, the tail being well clear of the loading van or truck. Aerovans have contributed to the export trade and are used by Belgian, French, Spanish and Swiss charter firms. First flown in January, 1945, the Aerovan has since been delivered in this country to Air Transport (Charter) Ltd. of Jersey ; Culliford Air Lines Ltd. of Blackpool ; East Anglian Flying Services of Southend; Patrick-Duval Aviation Services of Birmingham ; Sivewright Airways Ltd. of Manchester and Ulster Aviation Ltd. of Belfast.

S.I.A.I. MARCHETTI
S.M. 95.

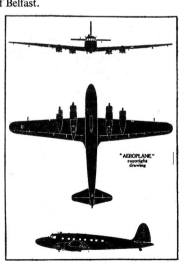

"AEROPLANE." copyright drawing

General Description.	Four-engine low-wing monoplane with single fin and rudder. Constructed by Societa Italiana Aeroplani Idrovolanti Marchetti, Sesto Calende, Italy.
Seating Capacity.	Crew of five and eighteen passengers.
Engines.	Four Alfa-Romeo, R.C.10, each of 930 h.p.
Dimensions.	Span : 112 ft. 5 ins. Length : 72 ft. 11 ins.
Performance.	Cruising speed : 186 m.p.h. Range : 2,113 miles.

S.I.A.I. MARCHETTI S.M. 95—*contd.*

Three-engine Savoia-Marchetti airliners were familiar sights at European airports before the war, being widely employed by the Belgian company S.A.B.E.N.A. as well as the Italian air lines. The S.M. 95 is the first Marchetti product to serve on the post-war Italian air routes. It was designed during the war period and one of the first examples built was seized by the German occupation forces and used by the *Luftwaffe*. After the Allied occupation of Italy another S.M. 95 was taken over by the R.A.F. and eventually used as a military transport aircraft between Great Britain and the Continent during 1945. The first post-war commercial versions of the S.M. 95 are in service with the Anglo-Italian company Alitalia and operate between Northolt Airport and Rome.

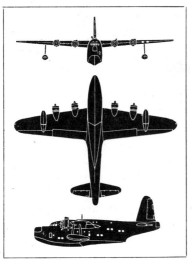

SHORT "HYTHE CLASS" FLYING-BOAT.

General Description. Four-engine high-wing monoplane flying-boat with single fin and rudder. Constructed by Short Brothers and Harland Ltd., Belfast and Rochester.

Seating Capacity. Crew of six and twenty-two passengers or sixteen sleeper berths.

Engines. Four Bristol Pegasus 48, each of 1,000 h.p.

Dimensions. Span : 112 ft. 9 ins. Length : 85 ft. 6 ins.

Performance. Cruising speed : 178 m.p.h. Range : 1,400 miles.

The tradition of using flying-boats on the Empire routes was inherited by B.O.A.C. from Imperial Airways which introduced the fleet of "Empire" flying-boats in 1936. The famous Sunderland flying-boat of the R.A.F. is merely a militarized version of the original "Empire" boats. "Empire" flying-boats served with distinction on the war-time routes of B.O.A.C. but, inevitably, many were lost due to war hazards, and in 1943 it was decided to augment the flying-boat fleet with a number of Sunderland III's originally laid down as transports for the R.A.F. Eventually twenty-four Sunderlands were delivered to B.O.A.C., of which seventeen now remain in service, the name of "Hythe Class" being bestowed in 1946 when extra civilian comforts were added to the internal furnishings. The faired-in turret in the bows of the "Hythe" boats betray their military derivation. B.O.A.C. now plans to dispose of the "Hythe" flying-boats and replace them on the Australian route with the five new Constellation landplanes recently purchased from Ireland. Two "Hythes" have already been sold to a British charter company.

SHORT "PLYMOUTH CLASS" FLYING-BOAT.

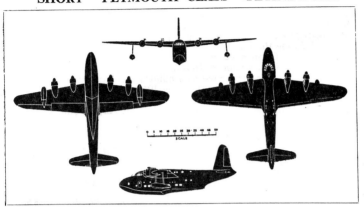

General Description.	Four-engine high-wing flying-boat with single fin and rudder. Constructed by Short Brothers and Harland Ltd., Belfast and Rochester.
Seating Capacity.	Crew of six and twenty-two passengers, or sixteen sleeper berths.
Engines.	Four Bristol Pegasus 38, each of 1,030 h.p.
Dimensions.	Span : 112 ft. 9 ins. Length : 85 ft. 4 ins.
Performance.	Cruising speed : 184 m.p.h. Range : 1,600 miles.

Unlike the "Hythe" boats, the "Plymouth Class" aircraft were designed from the outset as civil airliners. Though fundamentally the same as the Sunderland in construction, the "Plymouths" have luxurious interior accommodation and can be distinguished from the "Hythes" by the streamlined nose and tail in place of the angular, sealed turrets. "Plymouth" is the B.O.A.C. name for the aircraft, the manufacturer's name being Sandringham V. Sandringhams have been sold abroad, and serve with airlines in Norway, New Zealand and South America. The first Sandringham flew in November, 1945. B.O.A.C.'s eight "Plymouth" boats operate from Berth 50, Southampton, on the "Dragon" Route to India, Hong Kong and Japan.

SHORT SOLENT.

General Description.	Four-engine high-wing monoplane flying-boat with single fin and rudder. Constructed by Short Brothers and Harland Ltd., Belfast and Rochester.
Seating Capacity.	Crew of seven and thirty passengers or twenty-four sleeper berths.
Engines.	Four Bristol Hercules 637, each of 1,690 h.p.
Dimensions.	Span : 112 ft. 9 ins. Length : 89 ft. 6 ins.
Performance.	Cruising speed : 240 m.p.h. Range : 2,300 miles.

Latest of the series of Short flying-boats to go into service on British Empire routes, the Solent commenced to replace landplane Yorks on the route to Johannesburg in May, 1948. Yorks had been operating

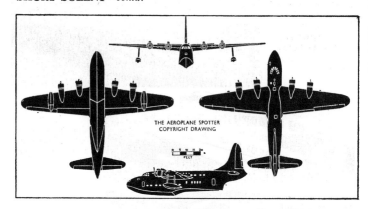

THE AEROPLANE SPOTTER
COPYRIGHT DRAWING

the "Springbok" service since the end of the war, but with the introduction of the Solent this route is once again flown by flying-boats as
it was pre-war by "Empire" aircraft. B.O.A.C. is almost alone in
world airlines in offering the increased comfort of the flying-boat on
trunk routes, though a considerable sacrifice in speed is inevitable. Many
contend that the airline traveller wants speed first and foremost and the
popularity or otherwise of the new Solent service will prove an interesting
test case of this vexed question. Derived from the military Seaford, a
development of the Sunderland, the Solent was first launched at Rochester
in December, 1946. It can readily be distinguished from the other Short
flying-boats by the existence of the curved fairing sweeping down from the
fin to the hull.

VICKERS VIKING

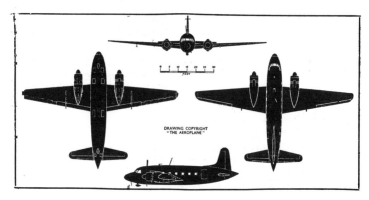

DRAWING COPYRIGHT
"THE AEROPLANE"

Douglas Dakota G-AIWE of Air Contractors Ltd. Air Contractors Ltd. operate three Dakotas from Bovingdon Airport.

Beech Expediter of the French charter company Air Transport at Gatwick Airport.

De Havilland Rapide of Air Enterprises Ltd. at Gatwick Airport.

Avro Anson G-AIXU, one of the aircraft operated by British Air Transport Ltd. on the service to Cowes.

Miles Aerovan of Culliford Air Lines Ltd. visiting Gatwick Airport.

De Havilland Rapide of Island Air Services Ltd.
(*Photos:*
A. S. C. Lumsden

Morton Air Services Airspeed Consul at Croydon Airport.

De Havilland Dove of Olley Air Service Ltd. Olley operates internal routes to Newmarket and Cowes.

Miles Aerovan G-AJOI of Sivewright Airways Ltd., one of the largest charter operators in the North at Ringway Airport.

Douglas DC-4 Skymaster of Skyways Ltd., Dunsfold, operating to Bahrein under charter to B.O.A.C.

An Avro York of Skyways Ltd., G-AHFI, *Skyway*.

Silver City Airways Lancastrian G-AHBV owned by British Aviation Services.

(Photos:
A. S. C. Lumsden
& F. J. Martin

General Description.	Twin-engine mid-wing monoplane with single fin and rudder. Constructed by Vickers-Armstrong Ltd., Weybridge, Surrey.
Seating Capacity.	Crew of four and from twenty-one to twenty-seven passengers.
Engines.	Two Bristol Hercules 634, each of 1,690 h.p.
Dimensions.	Span : 89 ft. 3 ins. Length : 65 ft. 2 ins.
Performance.	Cruising speed : 210 m.p.h. Range : 1,700 miles.

First post-war British civil aircraft to be put into regular airline service, the Vickers Vikings with their red B.E.A. " Speed-Key " insignia are now as familiar on European air routes as were the old Handley-Page Heracles biplanes of Imperial Airways in the 'thirties. Developed initially from the notable Wellington bomber of the R.A.F., the first Viking flew in June, 1945.   Produced mainly for British European Air-ways, the Viking has also been sold to many foreign airlines including the Scandinavian Airlines System, Indian National Airways, Iraqi Air-ways, Central African Airways and South African Airways.   First scheduled flight by a B.E.A. Viking took place on 1st September, 1946, between Northolt and Copenhagen.   The first type of Viking in service with B.E.A. was the Mk. 1A which had a noticeably shorter nose than the present model, the Mk. 1B.   All the Viking 1A aircraft have now been withdrawn from scheduled services of B.E.A. in favour of the Viking 1B, of which type the Corporation now has its full fleet of thirty-five aircraft.

ASSOCIATE COMPANIES OF BRITISH EUROPEAN AIRWAYS OPERATING   INTERNAL   ROUTES   IN   GREAT   BRITAIN

Cardiff—Weston-super-Mare	Cambrian Air Services Ltd. Western Airways Ltd.
Carlisle—Isle of Man	Air Navigation & Trading Co. Manx Air Charters Ltd. [Ltd. Scottish Aviation Ltd. West Cumberland Air Services.
Croydon—Cowes	Air Enterprises Ltd. British Air Transport Ltd. Olley Air Services.
Croydon—Newmarket	Olley Air Services.
Birmingham—Isle of Man	Patrick-Duval Aviation Ltd.
Birmingham—Liverpool	Patrick-Duval Aviation Ltd.
Birmingham—Southampton	Patrick-Duval Aviation Ltd.
Newcastle—Isle of Man	Northern Air Charter Ltd.
Prestwick—Blackpool	Scottish Aviation Ltd.
Southampton—Cowes	Air Enterprises Ltd.
Yeadon—Isle of Man	Lancashire Aircraft Corporation

British Aircraft Manufacturers since 1908
Günter Endres   ISBN: 071102409X   235mm x 172mm   H/B   £16.99

British Airports Then & Now
Leo Marriott   ISBN: 0711020760   235mm x 172mm   H/B   £12.99

British Military Airfields Then & Now
Leo Marriott   ISBN: 0711025150   235mm x 172mm   H/B   £19.99

Classic Civil Aircraft: 1 Lockheed Constellation (reprint)
Kenneth Wixey   ISBN: 0711017352   235mm x 172mm   H/B   £14.99

Flights to Disaster
Andrew Brookes   ISBN: 0711024758   235mm x 172mm   H/B   £14.99

From the Flightdeck: 9 Toronto-Heathrow
Bruce Campion-Smith   ISBN: 0711022127   235mm x 172mm   P/B   £10.99

The Lady: Boeing B-17 Flying Fortress
Don Patterson   ISBN: 0711022151   292mm x 216mm   P/B   £9.99

Lancaster at War: 4 Pathfinder Squadron
Alex Thorne   ISBN: 0711018820   292mm x 216mm   H/B   £16.99

Lancaster at War: 5 Fifty Years On
Mike Garbett & Brian Goulding   ISBN: 0711023972   292mm x 216mm   H/B   £19.99

Luftwaffe in the Battle of Britain (reprint)
Armand van Ishoven   ISBN: 0711025762   292mm x 216mm   P/B   £14.99

Modern Civil Aircraft: 13 Boeing 727
Peter Gilchrist   ISBN: 0711020817   235mm x 172mm   P/B   £10.99

Postwar Military Aircraft: 4 Avro Vulcan
Andrew Brookes   ISBN: 0711015481   235mm x 172mm   H/B   £14.99

RAF Bomber Airfields of World War 2
Jonathan Falconer   ISBN: 0711020809   292mm x 216mm   H/B   £19.99

Swordfish Special (reprint)
W. A. Harrison   ISBN: 071100742X   292mm x 216mm   H/B   £12.99

First published 1948
This impression 1998

ISBN 0 7110 2583 5

Published by Ian Allan Publishing
an imprint of
Ian Allan Publishing Ltd, Terminal House, Station Approach, Shepperton,
Surrey TW17 8AS.
Printed by Ian Allan Printing Ltd, Riverdene, Molesey Road, Hersham,
Surrey KT12 4RG.

Code: 9804/B2